11/09

LADDERS to SUCCESS

on the State Assessment

LEVEL D

Mathematics

LEVELED INSTRUCTION AND PRACTICE ON 10 ESSENTIAL SKILLS

Po\11

PHOTO CREDITS

Page 13-Microbot on a Penny courtesy of Dartmouth College

Page 20-Comet in the Sky, © 2006 Jupiterimages Corporation

Page 27-Boy Brushing Teeth, Brand X Pictures/Royalty Free

Page 34-Boys Working Out on Dance-Dance Revolution, AP Photo/Gene J. Puskar

Page 41-Bundle of Letters, © 2006 Jupiterimages Corporation

Page 48-Fisherman Releasing Rainbow Trout, © Steve Bly/Alamy

Page 55-Cake Man Raven with Wedding Cake, Hiroko Masuike/The New York Times

Page 62-Chinese Vase, © 2006 Jupiterimages Corporation

Page 69-Terrier Licking Birthday Cupcake, © Gaetano Images Inc./Alamy

Page 76-Lion Kazo and Puppy Cairo, AP Photo/Today's Local News, Christian Calabria

Page 83-Bald Eagle, © 2006 Jupiterimages Corporation

Page 90-Papyrus of Artemidorus, AP Photo/Massimo Pinca

Page 97-Experimental Flying Car, © Corbis

Page 104-Still from "The Curse of the Were-Rabbit," Bureau L.A. Collection/Corbis

Page 111-Sydney Kids and Roboraptor, AP Photo/Rick Rycroft

Page 118-Person Playing the Cello, © Royalty-Free Corbis

Page 125-Girl Wearing Football Uniform, Chip Simons/Getty Images

Page 132-Eel City, Hawaii Undersea Research Lab. P.I.: Hubert Staudigel, Scripps Institution of Oceanography

Page 139-Full Earth, courtesy of NASA

Page 146-Rows of Athletic Shoes, © 2006 Jupiterimages Corporation

Ladders to Success, Mathematics Level D
184NA
ISBN-10: 1-59823-466-8
ISBN-13: 978-1-59823-466-4

Cover Illustration: Sam Ward/Mendola Artists

Triumph Learning® 136 Madison Avenue, 7th Floor, New York, NY 10016
Kevin McAllley, President and Chief Executive Officer

© 2007 Triumph Learning, LLC
A Haights Cross Communications, Inc. company

Printed in the United States of America.

10 9 8 7 6

Table of Contents

Letter to the Student

Dear Student,

Welcome to **Ladders to Success** for Level D. This book will help you work on the ten math skills most important to you this year. There is one lesson for each skill. You will master all ten skills by working through all ten lessons one by one.

This book does not rush you through a skill. Each lesson is fourteen pages long. This gives you plenty of time to really get comfortable learning what each skill means. You will see how each skill works in math problems.

The first page of every lesson is called Show What You Know. Take this short quiz to see how much you know about a skill before digging into the lesson. The next section, Guided Instruction 1, will start you off with some friendly guided review and practice. Practice the Skill 1, which follows Guided Instruction 1, shows you how to answer a multiple-choice question before asking you to try more by yourself. The next section, News Flash, is an exciting news story. It also comes with an activity.

Following the first News Flash is a three-page section called Ladder to Success. This section will give you three chances to practice the skill. Each practice is a little harder as you go "up the ladder." Now you are ready for the second part of the lesson.

The second part of the lesson is just like the first. You will see Guided Instruction 2, Practice the Skill 2, and another News Flash. This time around these sections are a little harder. The last two pages of each lesson are called Show What You Learned. Show off everything you have learned in the lesson by correctly answering multiple-choice questions on the skill. Words that are boldfaced in the lessons appear in the glossary at the back of the book.

The lessons in this book will help you practice and improve your skills. They will also get you ready for the tests you will be taking this year. Some of the practice will be in the style of the state test. You will be answering multiple-choice and open-ended questions. You may see questions like these on your state test. Practicing with these types of questions will build your confidence.

We hope you will enjoy using Ladders to Success. We want you to climb the ladder to success this year. This book will help you get started!

Letter to the Family

Dear Parent or Family Member,

The **Ladders to Success** series of workbooks is designed to prepare your child to master ten of the fundamental skills in mathematics that are essential for success, both in the curriculum and on state tests. *Ladders to Success* provides guided review and practice for the skills that are the building blocks of your child's education in math. These are also the skills that will be tested on the state test in mathematics. Your child's success will be measured by how well he or she masters these skills.

Ladders to Success is a unique program in that each lesson is organized to ensure your child's success. Ten skills that students often find challenging are treated individually in ten lessons. Students are guided and supported through the first part of each lesson until they are ready to take on unguided practice in the second part of the lesson. Each lesson is fourteen pages long to give the student ample opportunity to review and practice a skill until a comfort level is reached. Support is gradually withdrawn throughout the lesson to build your child's confidence for independent work at the end of each lesson.

We invite you to be our partner in making learning a priority in your child's life. To help ensure success, we suggest that you review the lessons in this book with your child. You will see how each lesson gets subtly but progressively harder as you go along. While teachers will guide your child through the book in class, your support at home, added to the support of guided instruction and practice in the series, is vital to your child's comprehension.

We ask you to work with us this year to help your young student climb the ladder to success. Together, we can make a difference!

Letter to the Teacher

Dear Teacher,

Welcome to **Ladders to Success** in *Mathematics* for Level D. The *Ladders to Success* series of workbooks for mathematics is designed to prepare your students to master ten fundamental, grade-appropriate skills in math that are essential for success, both in the curriculum and on your state tests. *Ladders* provides guided review and practice for the skills that are the building blocks of the student's education. These are also skills that will be tested on your state tests in mathematics.

Ladders to Success is a unique program in that each lesson is leveled, or scaffolded, to ensure your students' success. Students are guided and supported through the first part of each lesson until they are ready to take on unguided practice in the second part of the lesson. Ten important skills are treated individually in ten lessons. Each lesson is fourteen pages long to give the student ample opportunity to review and practice a skill until a comfort level is reached. Support is slowly withdrawn throughout the lesson to build your students' confidence for independent work at the end of each lesson.

Ladders has a consistent, symmetrical format. The format is predictable from lesson to lesson, which increases students' comfort level with the presentation of skills-based information and practice. The first page of every lesson is called Show What You Know. This is a short diagnostic quiz to determine how much a student knows about a particular skill before digging into the lesson. It represents a snapshot of where each student is "now" before additional review and practice. This diagnostic quiz can be your guide in the way you choose to use the different parts of the lesson that follows.

The next section, Guided Instruction 1, will start students off slowly with guided review and practice. Practice the Skill 1, which immediately follows Guided Instruction 1, models how to answer a multiple-choice question before asking students to try more by themselves. The next section, News Flash, is an exciting contemporary news story that will engage students' interest. It is accompanied by an activity, often involving a math tool, under the heading Solve It.

Following the first News Flash is a three-page section called Ladder to Success, which embodies the spirit of the *Ladders* series. This section provides three more chances to practice the skill. What makes this section unique is that each practice is a little harder as students go "up the ladder." By the time students have finished the third practice, they are ready for the second part of the lesson, which mirrors the first part. The Ladder to Success section is the crucial bridge between the first part of the lesson and the second.

Thus, you will now see Guided Instruction 2, Practice the Skill 2, and another News Flash. This time around, however, these sections are more challenging. The problems are more difficult, and there is less modeling. The activity under the Solve It heading in the second News Flash in each lesson, for example, is an unscaffolded math activity.

The last two pages of each lesson represent a Posttest on the skill of the lesson. It is called Show What You Learned. This is the student's chance to show off everything he or she has learned in the lesson by successfully answering multiple-choice questions on the skill. The Posttest ends with an open-ended question, giving students the opportunity to show a deeper understanding of the skill now that they have completed the lesson. Words that are boldfaced in the lessons appear in the glossary at the back of the book.

Triumph Learning supports you in the difficult challenges you face in engaging your students in the learning process. *Ladders to Success* attempts to address some of these challenges by providing lessons that contain interesting material; scaffolded, or leveled, support; and a spectrum of multiple-choice questions and open-ended activities. This will allow students to build their confidence as they work toward proficiency with each skill in each lesson.

We ask you to work with us this year to help your students climb the ladder to success. Together, we *will* make a difference!

Show What You Know

Before you begin this lesson on multiplication, answer these questions. Choose the letter of the correct answer for each problem.

1. 40
  $\times\ 5$

What is the product?

A 2
B 20
C 200
D 2,000

2. $4 \times 6 = 24$

  $4 \times 60 = 240$

  $4 \times 600 = \boxed{}$

Which number is missing from the pattern?

A 240
B 2,400
C 24,000
D 240,000

3. $34 \times 2 = \boxed{}$

What is the product?

A 12
B 28
C 68
D 86

4. 68
  $\times\ 4$

What is the product?

A 224
B 242
C 264
D 272

5. $231 \times 3 = \boxed{}$

What is the product?

A 693
B 639
C 396
D 369

6. 482
  $\times\ 7$

What is the product?

A 2,864
B 2,874
C 3,364
D 3,374

Introduction

When you **multiply** numbers, you find the **product** of 2 or more groups that are the same size. You will use patterns and models to multiply.

Here's How

What is 40 × 3?

Think About It

You can use place-value models to show 3 groups of 40, or 3 groups of 4 tens.

Count by tens to find the product.

40 × 3 = 120

> 3 groups of 4 tens = 12 tens
> 12 tens = 1 hundred 2 tens
> 1 hundred 2 tens = 120

Try This Strategy

Use Patterns

Find 6 × 7,000.

You can multiply multiples of 10, 100, and 1,000 using **patterns**.

6 × 7 = 42	Think: 6 × 7 ones = 42 ones
6 × 70 = 420	Think: 6 × 7 tens = 42 tens
6 × 700 = 4,200	Think: 6 × 7 hundreds = 42 hundreds
6 × 7,000 = 42,000	Think: 6 × 7 thousands = 42 thousands

3 1833 05781 4680

Study the problem. Use the **Math Guide** for tips that can help you understand how to multiply a 2-digit **factor** by a 1-digit factor.

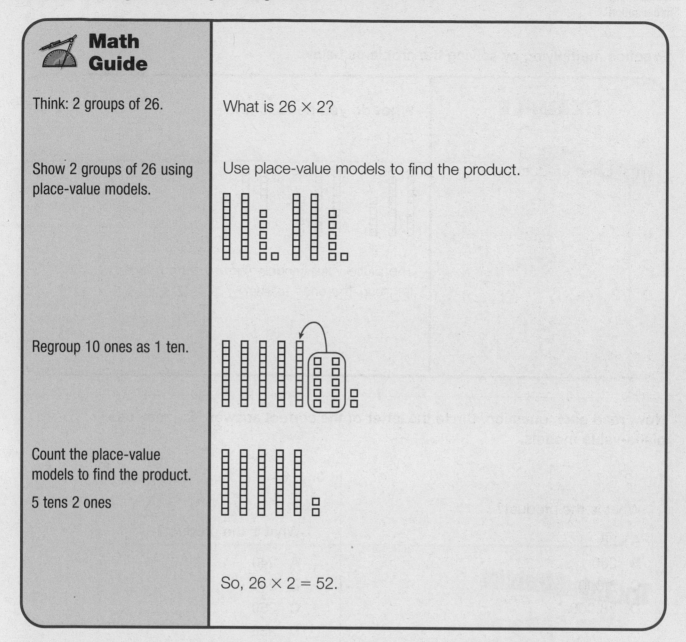

Math Guide

Think: 2 groups of 26.

What is 26 × 2?

Show 2 groups of 26 using place-value models.

Use place-value models to find the product.

Regroup 10 ones as 1 ten.

Count the place-value models to find the product.

5 tens 2 ones

So, 26 × 2 = 52.

Now, use what you already know and what you have learned to **multiply using place-value models and patterns.**

Answer the questions on the next page.

Practice the Skill 1

Practice multiplying by solving the problems below.

EXAMPLE

$24 \times 3 = \boxed{}$

What is the product?

A 12

B 42

C 62

D 72

What do you need to find?

Find 24×3.

The place-value models show 6 tens 12 ones. Regroup the ones to show 7 tens 2 ones.

Now, read each question. Circle the letter of the correct answer. You may use place-value models.

1. $40 \times 7 = \boxed{}$

What is the product?

A 28

B 280

C 2,800

D 28,000

2. $200 \times 6 = \boxed{}$

What is the product?

A 12

B 120

C 1,200

D 12,000

3. $\begin{array}{r} 64 \\ \times\ 4 \\ \hline \end{array}$

What is the product?

A 240

B 246

C 250

D 256

4. $13 \times 6 = \boxed{}$

What is the product?

A 78

B 72

C 70

D 68

The World's Smallest Robot

The robot is much smaller than the size of a penny.

Hanover, NH—Researchers have built the world's smallest robot. The robot is half the length of a period. About 200 of the robots could fit on the tip of a finger. These robots could someday help fix problems on small objects, like computer chips.

The robot has two parts that let it move. One lets it move forward and the other is for turning. The robot moves by crawling along like a worm. It turns by putting a "foot" onto the ground. Then, it spins like a bike rider skidding around a corner. The robot can move up to 20,000 steps a second!

Solve It

Use what you have learned about the robots to help you answer the questions below. Show your work on a separate sheet of paper.

1. Two hundred of the robots in the article could fit on the tip of a finger. How many of the world's smallest robots could fit on 6 fingers?

2. The robot moves 9,000 steps in a second. The robot moves at the same rate for 4 seconds. How many steps will it move in 4 seconds?

3. Four researchers each test 14 models of the robot. How many models do they test in all?

Ladder to Success

Review

You have learned how to multiply using patterns and models.

Review the methods you can use to multiply whole numbers.

- You can use patterns to multiply multiples of 10, 100, and 1,000.
- You can use place-value blocks to multiply a 2-digit number by a 1-digit number.

Practice 1

Jeremy studies for his science test 27 minutes each day for 3 days. How long does he spend studying for his science test?

What I Already Know	Jeremy studies 27 minutes each day for his science test. He studies for 3 days.
What I Need to Find Out	How long does he spend studying for his science test?
What I Need to Do	Multiply 27 by 3.

You can use place-value models to solve this problem.

Show 3 groups of 27.
Use the place-value models to
complete the statements.

The models show _____ tens and _____ ones.

Regroup _____ ones to _____ tens _____ ones.

How long does Jeremy spend studying for his science test? _____

20 ones = 2 tens

---

1. 38 × 6 = ☐

What is the product?

A 182   **C** 222

B 188   **D** 228

2.   81
     × 4

What is the product?

A 364   **C** 324

B 342   **D** 304

Practice 2

Tori collects stamps. She keeps her stamps in an album. Each page has 18 stamps on it. Her album has 7 pages. How many stamps does Tori have?

What I Already Know	Each page of the album has 18 stamps. The album has 7 pages.
What I Need to Find Out	How many stamps are in the album?
What I Need to Do	Find 18 × 7.

You could use place-value models to solve this problem. Another way to solve this problem is by using grid paper.

Draw and shade a rectangle that is 7 squares high and 18 squares wide.

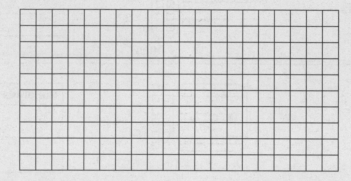

The number of shaded squares represents the product.

How many squares are inside the rectangle? _____

How many stamps are in the album? _____

1. 26 × 9 = ☐

   What is the product?

   A 1,836

   B 234

   C 224

   D 184

2.   31
     × 8

   What is the product?

   A 248

   B 241

   C 168

   D 32

Practice 3

There are 3 vans of people going on a field trip. Each van holds 14 people. How many people are going on the field trip?

Reread the problem to see what you need to do.

You need to find out how many people are going on the field trip. This means you should find 14 × 3.

How can you multiply 14 × 3?

You could use place-value models, but place-value models take a lot of time to use. You can multiply the numbers using paper and pencil.

Step 1
Model 3 groups of 14.
Multiply the ones.

3 × 4 ones

	Hundreds	Tens	Ones
×		1	4
			3
		1	2

Step 2
Multiply the tens.

3 × 1 ten

	Hundreds	Tens	Ones
×		1	4
			3
		1	2
		3	0

Step 3
Add to find the product.
Complete the problem.

	Hundreds	Tens	Ones
×		1	4
			3
		1	2
+		3	0
		☐	☐

How many people are going on the field trip? _____

How is using paper and pencil like using place-value models? How is it different?

_____

_____

You will build upon what you learned in Part 1 by learning to use paper and pencil to multiply whole numbers.

Find 53 × 7.

Think About It

You can use a place-value chart to multiply the numbers.

Step 1: Multiply the ones.

Step 2: Multiply the tens.

Step 3: Add to find the product.

	Hundreds	Tens	Ones
×		5	3
			7
		2	1	← 7 × 3 = 21
+	3	5	0	← 7 × 50 = 350
	3	7	1

So, 53 × 7 = 371.

Try This Strategy

Regroup as You Multiply
Find 35 × 6.

Step 1 Multiply the ones. Regroup if necessary.	**Step 2** Multiply the tens. Add all the tens.
3 35 × 6 ‾‾‾ 0 6 × 5 ones = 30 ones	3 35 × 6 ‾‾‾ 210 6 × 3 tens = 18 tens 18 tens + 3 tens = 21 tens 21 tens = 2 hundreds 1 ten

Study the problem. Use the **Math Guide** for tips that can help you understand how to multiply a 3-digit number by a 1-digit number.

 Math Guide

Be sure to regroup as necessary in each step.

For the tens and hundreds, always check for regrouped numbers.

Be sure to multiply *each* digit in the 3-digit factor by the 1-digit factor.

Find 187 × 4.

Step 1	**Step 2**	**Step 3**
Multiply the ones. Regroup if necessary.	Multiply the tens. Add all the tens. Regroup if necessary.	Multiply the hundreds. Add all the hundreds.
$\begin{array}{r} 2 \\ 187 \\ \times\ \ 4 \\ \hline 8 \end{array}$	$\begin{array}{r} 3\,2 \\ 187 \\ \times\ \ 4 \\ \hline 48 \end{array}$	$\begin{array}{r} 3\,2 \\ 187 \\ \times\ \ 4 \\ \hline 748 \end{array}$
4 × 7 ones = 28 ones 28 ones = 2 tens 8 ones	4 × 8 tens = 32 tens 32 tens + 2 tens = 34 tens 34 tens = 3 hundreds 4 tens	4 × 1 hundred = 4 hundreds 4 hundreds + 3 hundreds = 7 hundreds

Round 187 to the nearest hundred.

Then, use patterns or mental math to multiply 200 × 4.

Estimate to check for reasonableness.

187 × 4
↓   ↓
200 × 4 = 800

Eight hundred is close to 748, so the answer is reasonable.

Now, use what you already know and what you learned to **multiply using paper and pencil.**

Answer the questions on the next page.

Practice the Skill 2

Choose the correct answer.

1. $73 \times 6 = \boxed{}$

   What is the product?

   A 428

   B 438

   C 448

   D 538

2. $\begin{array}{r} 47 \\ \times\ 6 \\ \hline \end{array}$

   What is the product?

   A 282

   B 242

   C 202

   D 182

3. $529 \times 3 = \boxed{}$

   What is the product?

   A 567

   B 587

   C 1,567

   D 1,587

4. $\begin{array}{r} 321 \\ \times\ \ 2 \\ \hline \end{array}$

   What is the product?

   A 624

   B 642

   C 742

   D 764

5. Gel markers come in packs of 24. Mrs. McGuire buys 5 packs of gel markers. How many gel markers does she buy in all?

   A 96 markers

   B 100 markers

   C 120 markers

   D 124 markers

6. The movie theater held 274 people. The 3 evening shows were sold out. How many people saw the evening shows in all?

   A 612 people

   B 622 people

   C 812 people

   D 822 people

Ice Found on Comet's Surface

Pasadena, CA—NASA recently crashed a space probe into a comet to study comets. The probe, *Deep Impact*, now sends data back to NASA.

Data sent from *Deep Impact* has already taught researchers a lot about comets. Comets are surrounded by a cloud of dust and ice particles. Researchers wondered where the ice particles came from. Data from *Deep Impact* showed scientists that some ice comes from the surface of the comet, but most comes from below the surface.

Researchers think that geyser-like blasts of dust and ice vapor shoot out from the comet. This dust and ice then makes up most of the cloud around the comet. Researchers hope *Deep Impact* will help them learn more about comets.

Solve It

Imagine you are a researcher studying comets as you answer these questions. Show your work on a separate sheet of paper.

1. *Deep Impact* sends data to NASA once each hour, or 24 times each day. How many times does *Deep Impact* send data to NASA in 7 days?

2. *Deep Impact* found 3 areas of ice on the comet's surface. At each area, *Deep Impact* collected 124 grams of ice to study. How many grams of ice did *Deep Impact* collect in all?

Show What You Learned

Now that you have practiced multiplying whole numbers, take this quiz to show what you have learned. Choose the letter of the correct answer for each problem.

1. 60
$\times$ 3

What is the product?

A 18

B 180

C 1,800

D 18,000

2. $7 \times 3 = 21$

$7 \times 30 = 210$

$7 \times 300 = \boxed{}$

$7 \times 3,000 = 21,000$

Which number is missing from the pattern?

A 210

B 2,100

C 21,000

D 210,000

3. $93 \times 4 = \boxed{}$

What is the product?

A 327

B 362

C 372

D 3,612

4. 53
$\times$ 8

What is the product?

A 324

B 404

C 414

D 424

5. $168 \times 5 = \boxed{}$

What is the product?

A 840

B 804

C 800

D 480

6. 696
$\times$ 2

What is the product?

A 1,282

B 1,292

C 1,382

D 1,392

7. 39
   × 6

What is the product?

A 184

B 186

C 234

D 236

8. 512 × 3 = ☐

What is the product?

A 1,536

B 1,546

C 1,636

D 1,646

9. 845
   × 5

What is the product?

A 4,425

B 4,225

C 4,025

D 4,005

10. The library has 228 books on each of 6 shelves. How many books are on all 6 shelves?

A 1,228 books

B 1,268 books

C 1,328 books

D 1,368 books

11. A container of juice holds 64 ounces. How many ounces of juice will 4 containers hold?

A 156 ounces

B 206 ounces

C 246 ounces

D 256 ounces

Show your work on a separate sheet of paper.

12. How is multiplying a 2-digit number by a 1-digit number the same as multiplying a 3-digit number by a 1-digit number? How is it different?

Show What You Know

Before you begin this lesson on division, answer these questions. Choose the letter of the correct answer for each problem.

1. $80 \div 4 = \square$

   What is the answer?

   A   2
   B   20
   C   200
   D   320

2. $18 \div 3 = 6$

   $180 \div 3 = 60$

   $1{,}800 \div 3 = \square$

   Which number is missing from the pattern?

   A   60
   B   600
   C   6,000
   D   60,000

3. $38 \div 2 = \square$

   What is the answer?

   A   76
   B   41
   C   19
   D   14

4. $4\overline{)58}$

   What is the answer?

   A   12
   B   14
   C   14 R1
   D   14 R2

5. $912 \div 4 = \square$

   What is the answer?

   A   206
   B   218
   C   228
   D   251

6. $7\overline{)893}$

   What is the answer?

   A   127 R4
   B   126 R4
   C   120 R3
   D   110 R3

Introduction

When you **divide** numbers, you find how many are in each group or how many groups there are. You will first use **patterns** and models to help you understand division.

Here's How

What is 120 ÷ 3?

Think About It

You can use place-value models to show how to divide 120 into 3 equal groups.

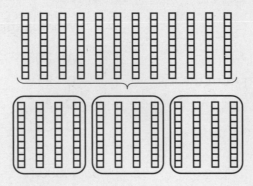

Count the number of tens in 1 group to find the **quotient**.

120 ÷ 3 = 40

120 = 12 tens
12 tens ÷ 3 = 4 tens
4 tens = 40

Try This Strategy

Use Patterns
Find 6,000 ÷ 2.

You can divide multiples of 10, 100, and 1,000 using patterns.

6 ÷ 2 = 3	Think: 6 ones ÷ 2 = 3 ones
60 ÷ 2 = 30	Think: 6 tens ÷ 2 = 3 tens
600 ÷ 2 = 300	Think: 6 hundreds ÷ 2 = 3 hundreds
6,000 ÷ 2 = 3,000	Think: 6 thousands ÷ 2 = 3 thousands

Study the problem. Use the **Math Guide** for tips that can help you understand how to divide a 2-digit number by a 1-digit number.

Math Guide	What is 72 ÷ 3?
Show 72 using 7 tens and 2 ones with place-value models.	Use place-value models to find the quotient. 
Divide the tens into 3 equal groups. Then, regroup the extra tens and ones to 12 ones.	
Divide the ones evenly into each group.	
Count the number of place-value models in 1 group to find the quotient. 2 tens 4 ones	So, 72 ÷ 3 = 24.

Now, use what you already know and what you learned to **divide using place-value models and patterns.**

Answer the questions on the next page.

Practice the Skill 1

Practice dividing by solving the problems below.

<table>
<tr><td>

EXAMPLE

4)56

What is the answer?

A 11

B 12

C 13

D 14

</td><td>

What do you need to find?

Find 56 ÷ 4.

The place-value models show 4 groups. Each group has 1 ten and 4 ones.

</td></tr>
</table>

Now, read each question. Circle the letter of the correct answer. You may use place-value models.

1. 640 ÷ 8 = ☐

What is the answer?

  A 8

  B 80

  C 800

  D 8,000

2. 56 ÷ 8 = 7

560 ÷ 8 = ☐

5,600 ÷ 8 = 700

Which number is missing from the pattern?

  A 7,000

  B 700

  C 70

  D 7

3. 8)96

What is the answer?

  A 12

  B 13

  C 14

  D 15

4. 98 ÷ 2 = ☐

What is the answer?

  A 44

  B 45

  C 47

  D 49

Brushing for a World Record

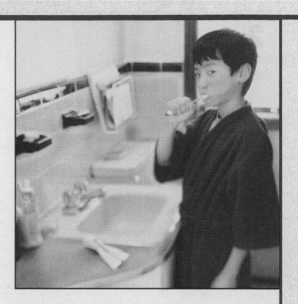

Manila, Philippines—Almost 11,000 children brushed their teeth at a park in Manila. The activity had two goals. The first was to break the world record for tooth brushing. The second was to teach children about brushing their teeth.

The children brushed their teeth for 3 minutes. As they brushed, dentists helped show them the correct way to brush their teeth. After they brushed their teeth, children tossed red caps into the air to celebrate.

The previous world record was set by 10,240 students in China. The children in the Philippines hope there were enough people brushing to break the world record.

Solve It

Imagine you are watching the tooth brushing event as you answer the questions below. Show your work on a separate sheet of paper.

1. Four hundred children are divided into 8 equal groups for the event. How many children are in each group?

2. One school brought 240 children to the event. They brought an equal number of children from each grade. The school has 6 grades. How many children came from each grade?

3. Each child brushed his or her teeth for 3 minutes. One group of children says that they brushed their teeth for 81 minutes in all. How many children are in the group?

Ladder to Success

Review

You have learned how to divide using patterns and models.

Review the methods you can use to divide whole numbers.

- You can use patterns to divide multiples of 10, 100, and 1,000.
- You can use place-value models to divide a 2-digit number by a 1-digit number.

Practice 1

It takes Carol 4 minutes to bike one mile. She bikes for 80 minutes. How many miles does she bike?

What I Already Know	It takes Carol 4 minutes to bike one mile. She bikes for 80 minutes.
What I Need to Find Out	How many miles does she bike?
What I Need to Do	Divide 80 by 4.

You can use place-value models to solve this problem.

Use the place-value models shown to complete the statements.

The models show _____ groups of tens.

Each group has _____ tens in it.

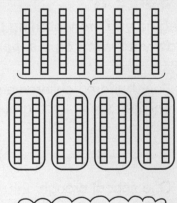

20 ones = 2 tens

How many miles does Carol bike? _____

---

1. 76 ÷ 2 = ☐

What is the answer?

A 48   **C** 33

B 38   **D** 23

2. 4)68

What is the answer?

A 12   **C** 16

B 13   **D** 17

Practice 2

Martin started to arrange his pictures in an album. He has placed the same number of pictures on each page. So far he has arranged 91 of his pictures on 7 pages of his album. How many pictures are on each page?

What I Already Know	Martin has arranged 91 of his pictures. He has used 7 pages of his album.
What I Need to Find Out	How many pictures are on each page?
What I Need to Do	Find 91 ÷ 7.

You can use place-value models to solve this problem.

In the space, draw how to divide the place-value models to show 91 ÷ 7.

Use **|** to show each tens place-value model and use **x** to show each ones place-value model.

Use your drawing to complete the statements.

In each group there is _____ ten and _____ ones.

How many pictures are on each page? _____

---

1. 92 ÷ 2 = ☐

What is the answer?

A 46

B 41

C 40

D 31

2. 3)‾54‾

A 11

B 16

C 18

D 28

Practice 3

Rosalie has 79 flowers. She makes 4 arrangements with the same number of flowers in each arrangement. How many flowers will each arrangement have? How many will be left over?

Reread the problem to see what you need to do.

You need to find out how many flowers will be in each arrangement and how many flowers are left over. This means you should find 79 ÷ 4.

How can you divide 79 by 4?

You could use place-value models but they take a lot of time to use. You can divide the numbers using paper and pencil.

Step 1
Model 79.
Divide the tens into
4 equal groups.

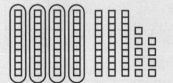

$$\begin{array}{r} 1 \\ 4\overline{)79} \\ -4 \\ \hline 3 \end{array}$$

← 1 ten in each group
← 4 tens used
← 3 tens left

Step 2
Regroup the
extra tens and
ones to 39 ones.

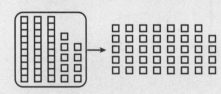

$$\begin{array}{r} 1 \\ 4\overline{)79} \\ -4\downarrow \\ \hline 39 \end{array}$$

← bring down 9 ones

Step 3
Divide the ones
evenly into
each group.

The left over ones
are the **remainder**.

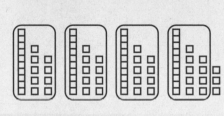

$$\begin{array}{r} 19 \\ 4\overline{)79} \\ -4 \\ \hline 39 \\ -36 \\ \hline 3 \end{array}$$

← 9 ones in each group

← 36 ones used
← 3 ones left

Write the quotient like this: 19 R3

How many flowers will each arrangement have? _____

How many will be left over? _____

How is using paper and pencil like using place-value models? How is it different?

_____

_____

You will build upon what you learned in Part 1 by learning to use paper and pencil to divide greater whole numbers.

What is $82 \div 6$?

Think About It

You can use paper and pencil to divide the numbers.

Divide the tens.	Bring down the ones. Divide the ones.
$\begin{array}{r} 1 \\ 6\overline{)82} \\ -\ 6 \\ \hline 2 \end{array}$ ← Multiply 1 × 6. ← Subtract 8 − 6. Compare 2 < 6.	$\begin{array}{r} 13\ \text{R4} \\ 6\overline{)82} \\ -\ 6\downarrow \\ \hline 22 \\ -\ 18 \\ \hline 4 \end{array}$ ← Bring down 2 ones. ← Multiply 3 × 6. ← Subtract 22 − 18. Compare 4 < 6.

So, $82 \div 6 = 13$ R4.

Estimate Quotients
Estimate $124 \div 6$.

Use **compatible numbers** to estimate quotients. Compatible numbers are numbers that are close to the original number and easy to divide mentally.

124 is close to 120.

$120 \div 6 = 20$

So, $124 \div 6$ is about 20.

Study the problem. Use the **Math Guide** for tips that can help you understand how to divide a 3-digit number by a 1-digit number.

 Math Guide

Find 284 ÷ 3.

Decide where to place the first digit in the quotient.

Step 1

$$3\overline{)284}$$

3 > 2: not enough hundreds
3 < 28: enough tens—the first digit is in the tens place

Divide the tens.

Step 2

$$\begin{array}{r} 9 \\ 3\overline{)284} \\ -27 \\ \hline 1 \end{array}$$

3 × 10 = 30 too big
3 × 9 = 27 good

Bring down the ones.

Divide the ones.

The leftover ones are the remainder.

Step 3

$$\begin{array}{r} 94\ R2 \\ 3\overline{)284} \\ -27\downarrow \\ \hline 14 \\ -12 \\ \hline 2 \end{array}$$

2 < 3; 2 is the remainder

Estimate to check for reasonableness using compatible numbers.

284 ÷ 3

300 ÷ 3 = 100

One hundred is close to 94 R2, so the answer is reasonable.

Now, use what you already know and what you learned to **divide using paper and pencil.**

Answer the questions on the next page.

Practice the Skill 2

Choose the correct answer.

1. Which is the best estimate for 315 ÷ 4?

   A 80

   B 70

   C 60

   D 50

2. $6\overline{)74}$

   What is the answer?

   A 10 R4

   B 12 R1

   C 12 R2

   D 12 R5

3. 620 ÷ 5 = ☐

   What is the answer?

   A 104

   B 124

   C 140

   D 144

4. 468 ÷ 5 = ☐

   What is the answer?

   A 91 R3

   B 92 R8

   C 93 R3

   D 94 R1

5. There are 276 campers at Camp Daybreak. Each tent sleeps 6 campers. How many tents are needed for all of the campers?

   A 46 tents

   B 44 tents

   C 42 tents

   D 41 tents

6. A florist has 165 flowers. She wants to use the same number of flowers in 7 arrangements. How many flowers will she have left over?

   A 1 flower

   B 2 flowers

   C 3 flowers

   D 4 flowers

Video Games in Gym Class

Charleston, WV—Students in West Virginia will soon use video games during gym classes. Students will be able to use the Dance Dance Revolution (DDR) video game as part of their gym classes.

Students are excited about the idea. DDR is a game where students step on a mat as they follow on-screen dance moves. Over time, the moves become faster and more difficult. Teachers are also excited about adding DDR to their classes. They hope the game will teach students that exercise can be fun and can happen in many different ways.

Solve It

Imagine that you are one of the students in the DDR gym class as you answer the questions below. Show your work on a separate sheet of paper.

1. A school spent $1,206 to buy 9 DDR stations. How much did each station cost?

2. The gym teacher has 48 DDR stations. She sets them in rows with 9 stations in each row. How many complete rows will she have? How many stations will be in the last row?

Show What You Learned

Now that you have practiced dividing whole numbers, take this quiz to show what you have learned. Choose the letter of the correct answer for each problem.

1. $90 \div 3 = \boxed{}$

What is the answer?

A 3

B 30

C 300

D 270

2. $63 \div 7 = 9$

$630 \div 7 = \boxed{}$

$6{,}300 \div 7 = 900$

Which number is missing from the pattern?

A 90

B 900

C 9,000

D 90,000

3. $68 \div 2 = \boxed{}$

What is the answer?

A 24

B 32

C 34

D 43

4. $5\overline{)92}$

What is the answer?

A 10 R2

B 14 R3

C 16 R2

D 18 R2

5. $936 \div 6 = \boxed{}$

What is the answer?

A 106

B 136

C 156

D 160

6. $80 \div 6 = \boxed{}$

What is the answer?

A 13 R2

B 12 R2

C 11 R2

D 10 R2

7. Which is the best estimate for 442 ÷ 9?

   A 40

   B 50

   C 60

   D 70

8. 5)78

What is the answer?

   A 11 R3

   B 12 R3

   C 14 R3

   D 15 R3

9. 674 ÷ 7 = ☐

What is the answer?

   A 90 R4

   B 92 R2

   C 96 R2

   D 98 R4

10. A baker makes 882 rolls. He puts them in bags with 6 rolls in each bag. How many bags of rolls does the baker make?

   A 93 bags

   B 109 bags

   C 112 bags

   D 147 bags

11. Mrs. Goswami made 223 cookies. She wants to make 6 cookie trays using the same number of cookies on each tray. How many cookies will she have left over?

   A 1 cookie

   B 2 cookies

   C 3 cookies

   D 4 cookies

Show your work on a separate sheet of paper.

12. Explain how you would find 262 ÷ 6 using paper and pencil.

Show What You Know

Before you begin this lesson on word problems, answer these questions. Choose the letter of the correct answer for each problem.

1. Angie writes the growth of a seedling in a table. If the seedling continues to grow at this rate, how tall will it be in the sixth week?

Seedling Growth	
Week	Growth (in cm)
1	0
2	2
3	4
4	6

   A 12 cm
   B 10 cm
   C 8 cm
   D 7 cm

2. Julie has 4 pets. Some of the pets are cats. Some of the pets are birds. Julie's pets have 10 legs in all. How many cats does Julie have?

   A 1 cat
   B 3 cats
   C 4 cats
   D 5 cats

3. The Chang family has 15 tomato plants, 9 cucumber plants, and 14 squash plants in their vegetable garden. How many tomato plants and squash plants do they have in their garden?

   A 23 plants
   B 24 plants
   C 29 plants
   D 38 plants

4. Each school van holds 9 people. How many vans are needed to take 75 people on a field trip?

   A 7 vans
   B 8 vans
   C 9 vans
   D 12 vans

5. Soccer practice is 45 minutes long. Soccer practice ends at 1:30 P.M. What time does soccer practice begin?

   A 12:15 P.M.
   B 12:45 P.M.
   C 1:45 P.M.
   D 2:15 P.M.

6. A family goes on a boat ride. There are 3 children and 2 adults. Children's tickets are $12 and adult tickets are $15. How much will the boat ride cost?

   A $27
   B $30
   C $36
   D $66

Introduction

It is important to follow a process, or plan, when you solve word problems. In Part 1, you will learn how to use and apply a four-step problem-solving process.

Here's How

Carrie found the masses of 4 objects during science class. Which object had the greatest mass?

Masses of Objects				
Object	A	B	C	D
Mass (in grams)	187	178	183	159

Think About It

Use the four-step problem-solving process.

READ Carefully read the problem. Identify important information.
I need to find the object with the greatest mass.

PLAN Make a plan for solving the problem.
I can compare the numbers in the table.

DO Follow your plan. Solve the problem.
187 > 183 > 178 > 159
So, 187 grams is the greatest mass.

CHECK Think of another way to check your answer.
I could place the masses on a number line and compare them.

Object A had the greatest mass, 187 grams.

Try This Strategy

Use a Pattern

Chairs were set up for a special event in the school gym. The first row had 3 chairs. The second row had 5 chairs. The third row had 7 chairs. The fourth row had 9 chairs. If this pattern continues, how many chairs will be in the sixth row?

Use a **pattern** to solve the problem. Each number in the pattern is 2 more than the previous number.

3, 5, 7, 9, <u>11</u>, <u>13</u>

There will be 13 chairs in the sixth row.

Study the problem. Use the Math Guide for tips that can help you understand how to choose an operation to solve a word problem.

 Math Guide

Read carefully to identify the question you need to answer.

A model airplane kit costs $51. Harry has $27 saved. How much more money does he need to save to buy the model airplane kit?

READ

What do you need to find out? You need to find out how much more money Harry needs to save to buy the model airplane kit.

What important information is in the problem? The model airplane kit costs $51. Harry has saved $27.

Key words can help you choose the operation. But understanding the word problem is the *best* way to choose the operation.

PLAN

Which operation can you use to solve this problem?

addition	used to join two or more groups
subtraction	used to separate a part from a whole or compare groups
multiplication	used to find out how many are in equal groups
division	used to find how many groups or how many in each group

Since you are comparing 2 groups, use subtraction.

Complete the operations carefully.

DO

$51
− $27
$24

You can use addition to check subtraction because they are **inverse operations**.

CHECK

$51 $24
− $27   + $27
$24 $51

The answer checks.

Now, use what you already know and what you learned to solve word problems.

Answer the questions on the next page.

Practice the Skill 1

LADDERS
to SUCCESS

LESSON
3
Word
Problems

Practice using the 4-step process by solving the problems below.

EXAMPLE

Sierra has 3 albums filled with pictures from her family vacations. Each album has 72 pictures in it. How many pictures are in all 3 albums?

A 24 pictures

B 75 pictures

C 176 pictures

D 216 pictures

READ **What do you need to find?**

Find how many pictures are in 3 albums.

PLAN **How will you solve the problem?**

Use multiplication.

DO

$$\begin{array}{r} 72 \\ \times\ 3 \\ \hline 216 \end{array}$$

CHECK **You can use repeated addition to check.**

$$\begin{array}{r} 72 \\ 72 \\ +\ 72 \\ \hline 216 \end{array}$$

Now, read each question. Circle the letter of the correct answer.

1. Kerri made beaded bracelets for her friends. She had 324 beads and used them all to make 9 bracelets. Each bracelet had the same number of beads. How many beads were on each bracelet?

   A 36 beads

   B 315 beads

   C 333 beads

   D 2,916 beads

2. Matt cuts several pieces of rope. The first piece of rope is 2 inches long, the second piece is 4 inches long, the third piece is 8 inches long, and the fourth piece is 16 inches long. If Matt continues to use this pattern, how long will the sixth piece of rope be?

   A 18 inches

   B 24 inches

   C 32 inches

   D 64 inches

Letters to Learn From

Clover Hill, VA—Students in Clover Hill do not just learn about history. They learn to be historians. Historians are people who study history.

The students take things that do not seem important and find out their history. Some students study letters that families wrote about soldiers who were away at war.

Students still read their history books about events that happened. But the teacher of the Clover Hill class thinks it is important that students learn what real people felt. Reading the letters of people who lived then is a great way to do this.

Solve It

Imagine that you are part of the Clover Hill history class. Show your work on a separate sheet of paper.

1. The Clover Hill High School has 3,000 letters from World War II. The students have read 1,387 of the letters. How many letters are left to read?

2. There are 64 students in the Clover Hill history class. The students work in 4 small groups to prepare a class project. Each group is the same size. How many students are in each group?

Ladder to Success

Review

You have learned how to use the four-step process to solve word problems.

Review the steps you can use to solve word problems.

- Follow the four-step process to read, plan, do, and check.
- Use patterns and choose the operation to solve problems.

Practice 1

At the end of the year, the fourth-grade class at Tanglewood School goes on a field trip. There are 138 students and adults going on the field trip. Each school van holds 8 people. How many school vans are needed for the field trip?

READ What I Already Know	There are 138 students and adults going on the field trip. Each school van holds 8 people.
PLAN What I Need to Find Out What I Need to Do	How many school vans are needed for the field trip? Use division to solve the problem.
DO	Complete the division problem. $8\overline{)138}$
CHECK	Show how to check your work.

The answer shows there are _____ full vans and _____ people left over.

You need to add 1 to the quotient, so there are enough seats for everyone.

How many school vans are needed for the field trip? _____

---

1. Tickets to the museum are $7 each. Madison has $59. What is the greatest number of tickets to the museum that Madison can buy?

   A 7 tickets   **C** 9 tickets
   B 8 tickets   **D** 10 tickets

2. There are 124 guests invited to a party. Each table at the party seats 8 people. How many tables are needed for the party?

   A 14 tables   **C** 16 tables
   B 15 tables   **D** 17 tables

Practice 2

It takes Jacob 45 minutes to ride his bike from his house to his grandparents' house. Jacob arrives at his grandparents' house at 4:00 P.M. What time did he leave his house?

READ **What I Already Know**	Jacob got to his grandparents' house at 4:00 P.M. The ride took him 45 minutes.
PLAN **What I Need to Find Out** **What I Need to Do**	What time did Jacob leave his house? I can work backward to solve the problem.
DO **Work Backward**	End time: 4:00 P.M. Elapsed time: [:] minutes → Time to ride to his grandparents' house. Start time: [:] P.M.
CHECK **Work Forward**	Start time: [:] P.M. Elapsed time: [:] minutes End time: [:] P.M.

What time did Jacob leave his house? _____

1. Sukrit bought a notebook for $2.25 and a binder for $5.60 at the store. He had $2.15 left after his purchases. How much money did Sukrit have when he went to the store?

   A $5.70
   B $7.85
   C $10.00
   D $12.00

2. Gina wants to get to practice 30 minutes early, so she can talk to her coach. If practice starts at 3:15 P.M., what time should Gina arrive at practice?

   A 2:30 P.M.
   B 2:45 P.M.
   C 3:45 P.M.
   D 4:15 P.M.

Practice 3

Hannah is playing a game where she spins the spinner shown and flips a coin. What are all of the possible outcomes of the game?

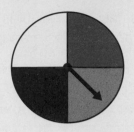

Reread the problem to see what you need to do.

You need to solve the problem to find out how many possible outcomes there are for the game.

How can you determine the number of possible outcomes?

One way to solve the problem is to draw a **tree diagram** that shows all of the possible outcomes for Hannah's game.

Study the start of the tree diagram below.

Complete the tree diagram by completing all of the branches to show the possible outcomes.

Spinner   **Coin Toss**

white   heads
               tails

red

gray

black

How many possible outcomes are there for Hannah's game? _____

How could you check your answer? _____

_____

_____

You will build upon what you learned in Part 1 by learning to solve more difficult word problems, including problems with extra information and multistep problems.

Here's How

The amusement park is open 12 hours each day during the summer. The roller coaster at the amusement park holds 24 passengers for each ride. In 1 hour, the roller coaster completes 9 rides. How many passengers can ride the roller coaster in 1 hour?

Think About It

Use the four-step problem-solving process.

READ Identify important information. Identify any extra information.
Important information: The roller coaster holds 24 passengers. In 1 hour it can complete 9 rides.
Extra information: The amusement park is open 12 hours each day.

PLAN Make a plan for solving the problem. I can multiply to solve the problem.

DO Follow your plan.
Solve the problem.

$$\begin{array}{r} 24 \\ \times\ 9 \\ \hline 216 \end{array}$$

CHECK How can you tell if your answer is reasonable?
I can use estimation to check my answer. 24 is close to 20. 9 is close to 10.
$20 \times 10 = 200$
200 is close to 216, so your answer is reasonable.

So, 216 passengers can ride the roller coaster in 1 hour.

Try This Strategy

Guess and Check

Tom bought a hat and a T-shirt for $30. The T-shirt cost $6 more than the hat. How much did the hat cost? How much did the T-shirt cost?

Guess and check to solve this problem.

Guess: $14 for the hat, $20 for the T-shirt
Check: $14 + $20 = $34
Since $34 > $30, try a lesser amount for the hat.

Guess: $12 for the hat, $18 for the T-shirt
Check: $12 + $18 = $30
Tom spent $12 for the hat and $18 for the T-shirt.

Study the problem. Use the **Math Guide** for tips that can help you understand how to solve a multistep word problem.

 Math Guide

An airline allows passengers to have bags that weigh up to 50 pounds at no extra charge. For each pound over 50 pounds, the airline charges $4. How much will a passenger have to pay for a bag that weighs 75 pounds?

Read carefully to understand the problem.

READ

What do you need to find out? You need to find out how much a passenger will pay for a bag that weighs 75 pounds.

What important information is in the problem? The airline only charges for each pound *over* 50 pounds. The bag weighs 75 pounds. The cost per pound is $4.

This is a multistep problem.

Decide how to solve each step, and in what order.

PLAN

Which operations can you use to solve this problem?

First, you need to subtract to find out how many pounds the passenger needs to pay for.

Then, you need to multiply to find how much the passenger will have to pay.

Complete the operations carefully.

DO

75 pounds − 50 pounds = 25 pounds

$$\begin{array}{r} 25 \\ \times \quad \$4 \\ \hline \$100 \end{array}$$

Remember to check *both* parts of the problem.

CHECK

Use inverse operations to check.

$100 ÷ $4 = 25

25 + 50 = 75

So, the passenger has to pay $100 for a 75-pound bag.

Now, use what you already know and what you learned to **solve word problems.**

Answer the questions on the next page.

Choose the correct answer.

1. It costs $15 per hour to rent a bike. A family rents 3 bikes. How much will they pay to rent the bikes for 5 hours?

   A $225

   B $205

   C $75

   D $45

2. Gretchen earns $25.50 babysitting. She then earns $7.25 raking the yard. Her brother also earns $8.50 for mowing the lawn. How much money did Gretchen earn in all?

   A $15.75

   B $31.25

   C $32.75

   D $41.25

3. Ty runs for 25 minutes each day. He then swims for 15 minutes each day. How many minutes does Ty run and swim in 6 days?

   A 60 minutes

   B 90 minutes

   C 150 minutes

   D 240 minutes

4. Lucy spends $38 on a helmet and knee pads for skateboarding. Her helmet cost $4 more than her knee pads. How much did her helmet cost?

   A $23

   B $21

   C $19

   D $17

5. Hector has a collection of 28 model cars and trucks. There are 16 model cars and 12 model trucks in his collection. How many model cars and trucks will be on each of 4 shelves if there is the same number of models on each shelf?

   A 3 models

   B 4 models

   C 6 models

   D 7 models

6. Which shows the correct order of the operations you need to use to solve the problem below?

   Tickets to the county fair cost $6 for children and $8 for adults. How much will it cost for 5 adults and 8 children to attend the county fair?

   A Multiply and then subtract.

   B Subtract and then multiply.

   C Multiply and then add.

   D Add and then multiply.

A Fish with Two Mouths?

Lincoln, NE—Clarence Olberding has many odd fishing stories. He has seen fish with missing fins. He has even seen fish with missing eyes. However, a recent catch was not like any he had seen before. This fish looked like it had two mouths!

At first people thought the second mouth was an adaptation. Researchers at Harvard University decided to study the fish. They found that the fish was injured when it was young. The injury made it appear that the fish had two mouths, but really it had just one.

Olberding was disappointed at what the researchers found. But, he was glad to have been a part of the experience.

Solve It

Think about what it would be like fishing in Nebraska as you answer the questions below. Show your work on a separate sheet of paper.

1. A group of 17 people went fishing on Holmes Lake in Nebraska. Each person caught 3 fish. The largest fish weighed 7 pounds. How many fish did the group catch?

2. A fisherman caught 2 fish. The fish weighed a total of 27 pounds. One fish weighed 3 pounds more than the other fish. How much did each fish weigh?

Show What You Learned

Now that you have practiced solving word problems, take this quiz to show what you have learned. Choose the letter of the correct answer for each problem.

1. There are 123 campers at Camp Sunrise. Each picnic table holds 8 campers. How many picnic tables are needed to seat all of the campers?

   A 14 picnic tables

   B 15 picnic tables

   C 16 picnic tables

   D 17 picnic tables

2. It takes Derek 45 minutes to walk from his house to his school. If Derek needs to be at school at 8:30 A.M., what time does he need to leave his house?

   A 7:15 A.M.

   B 7:45 A.M.

   C 8:15 A.M.

   D 8:45 A.M.

3. Addy built several towers using blocks. The table shows the number of blocks she used for each tower.

If she continues to build towers using this pattern, how many blocks will her sixth tower have?

Blocks Used for Towers	
Tower	**Blocks**
1	7
2	13
3	19
4	25

   A 26 blocks

   B 31 blocks

   C 37 blocks

   D 43 blocks

4. Quentin places pictures in an album. His album has 36 pages. He puts 4 photos on each page. How many photos does Quentin have in his album?

   A 144 photos

   B 124 photos

   C 116 photos

   D 104 photos

5. Percy buys a scarf and a hat at the store. He spends $12.40 on the scarf and $8.55 on the hat. He has $1.05 left when he leaves the store. How much money did Percy start with?

   A $20.00

   B $20.95

   C $21.00

   D $22.00

6. Kelly has 6 pets. She has some dogs and some birds. Her pets have 16 legs in all. How many birds does Kelly have?

   A 2 birds

   B 3 birds

   C 4 birds

   D 5 birds

7. The book store had a sale. All hardcover books were on sale for $12 each. All paperback books were on sale for $7 each. Mason bought 3 hardcover books and 2 paperback books at the sale. How much did he spend in all?

A $14

B $36

C $50

D $60

8. A florist used 184 flowers in 8 flower arrangements. Each arrangement had 5 yellow flowers. If each arrangement had the same number of flowers, how many flowers were in each arrangement?

A 18 flowers

B 23 flowers

C 28 flowers

D 40 flowers

9. Which shows the correct order of operations used to solve the problem below?

> A seniors group goes on a trip. They take 6 cars of 5 people each and 3 vans of 8 people each. How many people go on the trip?

A Multiply and then add.

B Add and then subtract.

C Multiply and then subtract.

D Add and then multiply.

10. Sally plays a game where she rolls a 1 to 6 number cube and flips 1 penny. How many possible outcomes are there for her game?

A 6 outcomes

B 8 outcomes

C 10 outcomes

D 12 outcomes

11. Tickets to a hockey game are $8 each. Mr. Fox has $62. What is the greatest number of tickets he can buy?

A 10 tickets

B 9 tickets

C 8 tickets

D 7 tickets

Show your work on a separate sheet of paper.

12. Read the problem below. Describe the strategy you will use to solve the problem. Then, solve the problem using that strategy.

Kanye records the temperature each hour. His measurements for the first 4 hours are 58°F, 62°F, 66°F, and 70°F. If the temperature continues to increase at this rate, what will the temperature be for hour 7?

Before you begin this lesson on equivalent fractions, answer these questions. Choose the letter of the correct answer for each problem.

1. Which fraction is equivalent to $\frac{3}{4}$?

   A $\frac{3}{8}$

   B $\frac{3}{6}$

   C $\frac{6}{8}$

   D $\frac{9}{10}$

2. $\frac{1}{2} = \frac{4}{\square}$

   What is the missing number?

   A 2

   B 4

   C 6

   D 8

3. Which statement is true?

   A $\frac{1}{3} = \frac{3}{1}$

   B $\frac{8}{12} = \frac{2}{3}$

   C $\frac{2}{4} = \frac{1}{4}$

   D $\frac{6}{8} = \frac{2}{3}$

4. Which fraction is equivalent to the fraction shown in the picture?

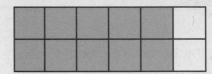

   A $\frac{2}{3}$

   B $\frac{3}{4}$

   C $\frac{4}{5}$

   D $\frac{5}{6}$

5. $\frac{3}{12} = \frac{\square}{4}$

   What is the missing number?

   A 1

   B 2

   C 3

   D 4

6. Which shows $\frac{4}{12}$ written in simplest form?

   A $\frac{1}{2}$

   B $\frac{5}{6}$

   C $\frac{1}{3}$

   D $\frac{1}{6}$

Guided Instruction 1

When you find **equivalent fractions**, you are renaming **fractions**. You will first study how to find equivalent fractions using models.

What fraction is equivalent to $\frac{1}{2}$?

Think About It

You can use fraction strips to find equivalent fractions.

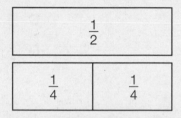

Compare the fraction strips. They are all the same size. This shows that the amounts are equivalent.

So, $\frac{1}{2}$ is equivalent to $\frac{2}{4}$.

Use Models

You can use other kinds of models to find equivalent fractions.

Find 2 fractions that are equivalent to $\frac{3}{4}$.

$$\frac{3}{4} \quad = \quad \frac{6}{8} \quad = \quad \frac{9}{12}$$

Study the problem. Use the **Math Guide** for tips that can help you understand how to find a missing number in an equivalent fraction.

 Math Guide

The box stands for a missing number.

What **numerator** makes this number sentence true?

$$\frac{1}{3} = \frac{\square}{12}$$

Use twelfths fraction strips because the **denominator** of the unknown fraction is 12.

You can use fraction strips to solve this problem.

Show $\frac{1}{3}$ with fraction strips. Then, place $\frac{1}{12}$ fraction strips until the strips are exactly the same length as $\frac{1}{3}$.

$\frac{1}{3}$			
$\frac{1}{12}$	$\frac{1}{12}$	$\frac{1}{12}$	$\frac{1}{12}$

Count the number of $\frac{1}{12}$ strips used to find the missing numerator.

So, $\frac{1}{3}$ is equivalent to $\frac{4}{12}$. The number 4 completes the number sentence.

Now, use what you already know and what you learned to find **equivalent fractions using models**.

Answer the questions on the next page.

Practice the Skill 1

Practice finding equivalent fractions by solving the problems below.

EXAMPLE

Which fraction is equivalent to $\frac{1}{2}$?

A $\frac{2}{3}$

B $\frac{6}{8}$

C $\frac{3}{4}$

D $\frac{5}{10}$

What do you need to find?

Find a fraction that is equivalent to $\frac{1}{2}$.

You can use fraction strips.

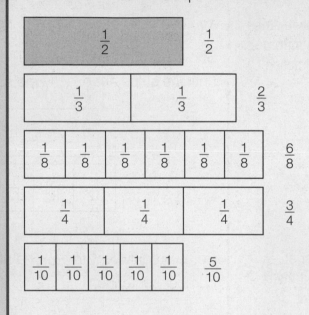

Now, read each question. Circle the letter of the correct answer. You may use fraction strips.

1. Which fraction is equivalent to $\frac{2}{3}$?

A $\frac{4}{6}$

B $\frac{2}{5}$

C $\frac{3}{4}$

D $\frac{5}{8}$

2. $\frac{1}{6} = \frac{\square}{12}$

What is the missing number?

A 1

B 2

C 3

D 4

Cake Man

Brooklyn, NY—Raven Dennis is the "Cake Man." He makes cakes that look like people, buildings, and motorcycles.

For the 120th birthday of the Brooklyn Bridge, Dennis baked a cake that was 7 feet tall! It took him five days to put the cake together. Three thousand people ate the cake. For a 16th birthday party, Dennis made a life-size cake of the birthday boy. The boy was amazed by how much the cake looked like him.

Dennis runs a bakery in Brooklyn, New York. His next cake will be a wedding cake with cages for doves built into it.

Solve It

Bakers often need to use equivalent measures in the kitchen. Imagine you are working alongside the Cake Man as you answer these questions. Show your work on a separate sheet of paper.

1. A frosting recipe calls for $\frac{3}{4}$ cup of powdered sugar. What is an equivalent amount of powdered sugar the Cake Man can use?

_____

2. The Cake Man needs $\frac{1}{2}$ cup of flour, but he only has a $\frac{1}{4}$-cup measure. How many $\frac{1}{4}$ cups will he need to use to equal $\frac{1}{2}$ cup?

_____

Ladder to Success

Review

You have learned how to find equivalent fractions.

Review the methods you can use to find equivalent fractions.

- You can use fraction strips to find equivalent fractions.
- You can use other models to find equivalent fractions.

Practice 1

Brooke found that Plant A grew $\frac{3}{4}$ inch in 1 week. She measured Plant B and found it grew the same amount. She recorded the growth of Plant B in eighths. What fraction did Brooke record for Plant B's growth?

What I Already Know	Plant A grew $\frac{3}{4}$ of an inch. Plant B grew the same amount. Plant B's growth was recorded in eighths.
What I Need to Find Out	What fraction with a denominator of 8 is equivalent to $\frac{3}{4}$?
What I Need to Do	Find a fraction equivalent to $\frac{3}{4}$ with a denominator of 8.

You can use fraction strips to solve the problem.

| $\frac{1}{4}$ | $\frac{1}{4}$ | $\frac{1}{4}$ | $\frac{3}{4}$ |

| $\frac{1}{8}$ | $\frac{1}{8}$ | $\frac{1}{8}$ | $\frac{1}{8}$ | $\frac{1}{8}$ | $\frac{1}{8}$ | $\frac{6}{8}$ |

What fraction did Brooke record for Plant B's growth? _____

How can you tell the fractions are equivalent? _____

_____

1. Which statement is true?

A $\frac{4}{5} = \frac{4}{10}$ C $\frac{4}{5} = \frac{8}{10}$

B $\frac{4}{5} = \frac{6}{10}$ D $\frac{4}{5} = \frac{9}{10}$

2. Which fraction is equivalent to $\frac{1}{3}$?

A $\frac{3}{1}$ C $\frac{1}{6}$

B $\frac{2}{3}$ D $\frac{3}{9}$

Practice 2

For a recipe, Lea needs $\frac{2}{3}$ cup of milk. The only measuring cup she can find is divided into twelfths. How many twelfths are equivalent to $\frac{2}{3}$?

What I Already Know	Lea needs $\frac{2}{3}$ cup of milk. Her measuring cup is divided into twelfths.
What I Need to Find Out	What fraction with a denominator of 12 is equivalent to $\frac{2}{3}$?
What I Need to Do	Find a fraction equivalent to $\frac{2}{3}$ with a denominator of 12.

You can use models to solve the problem.

First, shade the thirds model to show $\frac{2}{3}$.

Then, shade the twelfths model until the shading is equal to the $\frac{2}{3}$ model.

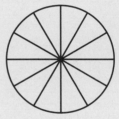

How many twelfths are equivalent to $\frac{2}{3}$? _____

How can you tell the fractions are equivalent?

_____

_____

---

1. Which fraction is equivalent to the fraction shown in the picture?

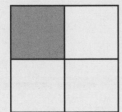

A $\frac{1}{5}$ C $\frac{3}{8}$

B $\frac{2}{8}$ D $\frac{3}{5}$

2. $\frac{3}{5} = \frac{\square}{10}$

A 2

B 4

C 6

D 8

Practice 3

Carol has 2 pieces of ribbon. The yellow piece of ribbon is $\frac{2}{3}$ inch long. The red piece of ribbon is $\frac{4}{8}$ inch long. Are the 2 pieces of ribbon the same length?

Reread the problem to see what you need to do.

You need to find out if the 2 pieces of ribbon are the same length. This means you need to find out if the fractions are equivalent.

How can you find if the fractions are equivalent?

You can shade models to determine if the fractions are equivalent.

Shade the circle to show $\frac{2}{3}$.

Shade the circle to show $\frac{4}{8}$.

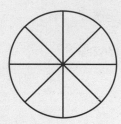

So, are the 2 pieces of ribbon the same length? _____

How can you tell? _____

_____

_____

You will build upon what you learned in Part 1 by learning to use multiplication and division to find equivalent fractions and show fractions in **simplest form**.

Here's How

Find 3 fractions that are equivalent to $\frac{4}{5}$.

Think About It

You could use fraction strips to find equivalent fractions. But you can also use multiplication to find equivalent fractions.

Multiply the numerator and the denominator of the fraction by the same number.

$\frac{4 \times 2}{5 \times 2} = \frac{8}{10}$	$\frac{4 \times 3}{5 \times 3} = \frac{12}{15}$	$\frac{4 \times 4}{5 \times 4} = \frac{16}{20}$

So, $\frac{4}{5} = \frac{8}{10} = \frac{12}{15} = \frac{16}{20}$.

Use Division

You can also find equivalent fractions using division.

Name a fraction that is equivalent to $\frac{8}{12}$.

Divide the numerator and the denominator by the same common factor.

$$\frac{8}{12} = \frac{8 \div 2}{12 \div 2} = \frac{4}{6}$$

So, $\frac{8}{12}$ is equivalent to $\frac{4}{6}$.

Study the problem. Use the **Math Guide** for tips that can help you understand how to write fractions in simplest form.

 Math Guide

So, 2 and 4 are the common factors.

What is the simplest form of $\frac{4}{12}$?

Find the common factors of the numerator and denominator.

Factors of 4: 1, 2, 4

Factors of 12: 1, 2, 3, 4, 6, 12

The **greatest common factor (GCF)** is the greatest factor common to 2 or more numbers.

So, 4 is the GCF of 4 and 12.

Be sure to divide **both** the numerator and denominator by the GCF.

Divide the numerator and the denominator by the GCF.

$$\frac{4}{12} = \frac{4 \div 4}{12 \div 4} = \frac{1}{3}$$

So, $\frac{4}{12}$ written in simplest form is $\frac{1}{3}$.

Now, use what you already know and what you learned to **write equivalent fractions**.

Answer the questions on the next page.

Practice the Skill 2

Choose the correct answer.

1. Which fraction is equivalent to $\frac{1}{6}$?

   A $\frac{2}{6}$

   B $\frac{2}{8}$

   C $\frac{2}{10}$

   D $\frac{2}{12}$

2. $\frac{3}{5} = \frac{9}{\square}$

   A 10

   B 15

   C 20

   D 25

3. Which shows $\frac{3}{9}$ written in simplest form?

   A $\frac{1}{3}$

   B $\frac{1}{5}$

   C $\frac{1}{6}$

   D $\frac{1}{9}$

4. Which statement is true?

   A $\frac{8}{16} = \frac{1}{5}$

   B $\frac{8}{16} = \frac{1}{4}$

   C $\frac{8}{16} = \frac{1}{3}$

   D $\frac{8}{16} = \frac{1}{2}$

5. For which fraction is $\frac{1}{3}$ the simplest form?

   A $\frac{6}{9}$

   B $\frac{5}{10}$

   C $\frac{9}{27}$

   D $\frac{6}{30}$

6. Pedro ate $\frac{3}{8}$ of a pizza. Lola ate the same amount of pizza. Which fraction represents the amount of pizza Lola ate?

   A $\frac{3}{16}$

   B $\frac{6}{16}$

   C $\frac{9}{16}$

   D $\frac{6}{8}$

Rare Vases Shattered by a Clumsy Visitor

Cambridge, England—Three 300-year-old vases were shattered by a clumsy museum visitor. The three Chinese vases were on display near a staircase in a museum. A visitor to the museum tripped on his shoelace and fell down the stairs. When he hit the display, the vases fell. As they hit the floor, the vases broke into very small pieces.

Another witness said it seemed like the man fell in slow motion as he tumbled toward the vases. Luckily, the visitor was not hurt by the fall.

The museum officials are determined to put the vases back together again—one piece at a time.

Solve It

Imagine that you are working on organizing the shattered pieces of the vases. Show your work on a separate sheet of paper.

1. A museum official has identified $\frac{8}{12}$ of the pieces for one vase. How can this fraction be shown in simplest form?

2. The base of another vase shattered into 100 pieces. So far, 50 pieces have been put back together. Write a fraction in simplest form that shows how many pieces have been put back together.

3. One vase had the image of a flower on it. The flower image broke into 15 pieces. So far, $\frac{1}{3}$ of the pieces have been put back together. Complete the statement below to show how many pieces have been put back together.

$$\frac{1}{3} = \frac{\boxed{}}{15}$$

Show What You Learned

Now that you have practiced finding equivalent fractions, take this quiz to show what you have learned. Choose the letter of the correct answer for each problem.

1. $\frac{4}{16} = \frac{1}{\square}$

What is the missing number?

A 2

B 4

C 8

D 12

2. Which fraction is equivalent to $\frac{5}{8}$?

A $\frac{2}{3}$

B $\frac{10}{8}$

C $\frac{10}{16}$

D $\frac{15}{16}$

3. Which statement is true?

A $\frac{8}{24} = \frac{1}{3}$

B $\frac{8}{24} = \frac{1}{4}$

C $\frac{8}{24} = \frac{1}{5}$

D $\frac{8}{24} = \frac{1}{6}$

4. Which fraction is equivalent to the fraction shown in the picture?

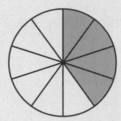

A $\frac{1}{5}$

B $\frac{1}{4}$

C $\frac{2}{3}$

D $\frac{2}{5}$

5. Which shows $\frac{10}{12}$ written in simplest form?

A $\frac{3}{4}$

B $\frac{5}{6}$

C $\frac{6}{7}$

D $\frac{7}{8}$

6. Casey drank $\frac{1}{2}$ of her juice. David drank the same amount of milk. Which fraction represents the amount of milk David drank?

A $\frac{5}{8}$

B $\frac{2}{5}$

C $\frac{9}{18}$

D $\frac{10}{16}$

7. $\frac{4}{5} = \frac{\square}{20}$

What is the missing number?

A 5

B 8

C 16

D 18

8. For which fraction is $\frac{5}{8}$ the simplest form?

A $\frac{8}{12}$

B $\frac{15}{24}$

C $\frac{24}{32}$

D $\frac{20}{40}$

9. Which fraction is equivalent to $\frac{9}{12}$?

A $\frac{3}{4}$

B $\frac{2}{3}$

C $\frac{1}{2}$

D $\frac{3}{8}$

10. What is the simplest form of $\frac{24}{64}$?

A $\frac{6}{16}$

B $\frac{12}{32}$

C $\frac{2}{5}$

D $\frac{3}{8}$

11. The Smith family ate $\frac{4}{16}$ of a pie one night for desert. The next night they ate the same amount of pie. Which fraction represents the amount of pie the Smith family ate the second night?

A $\frac{2}{8}$

B $\frac{1}{3}$

C $\frac{3}{4}$

D $\frac{1}{6}$

Show your work on a separate sheet of paper.

12. Cheung spends $\frac{8}{12}$ of an hour working on his book report. Toby spends $\frac{2}{3}$ of an hour working on his book report. Do Cheung and Toby spend the same amount of time working on their book reports? Explain your reasoning.

Show What You Know

Before you begin this lesson on adding and subtracting fractions, answer these questions. Choose the letter of the correct answer for each problem.

1. $\frac{1}{4} + \frac{1}{4} = \square$

   What is the sum?

   A $\frac{1}{8}$

   B $\frac{2}{8}$

   C $\frac{1}{2}$

   D $\frac{2}{2}$

2. What is $\frac{5}{8} - \frac{2}{8}$?

   A $\frac{3}{16}$

   B $\frac{3}{8}$

   C $\frac{7}{16}$

   D $\frac{7}{8}$

3. $\frac{1}{2} + \frac{3}{4} = \square$

   What is the sum?

   A $\frac{1}{4}$

   B $\frac{2}{3}$

   C $1\frac{1}{8}$

   D $1\frac{1}{4}$

4. Omar reads $\frac{1}{8}$ of his book on Saturday. On Sunday, he reads another $\frac{3}{8}$ of his book. How much of his book did he read in all on Saturday and Sunday?

   A $\frac{1}{2}$ of the book

   B $\frac{1}{3}$ of the book

   C $\frac{1}{4}$ of the book

   D $\frac{1}{5}$ of the book

5. Mrs. Wilson bought $\frac{1}{2}$ pound of turkey and $\frac{3}{4}$ pound of ham at the deli. How much more ham than turkey did Mrs. Wilson buy?

   A $\frac{1}{4}$ pound

   B $\frac{1}{2}$ pound

   C $\frac{2}{3}$ pound

   D $1\frac{1}{4}$ pounds

6. Sun walks $\frac{5}{6}$ mile on Monday. On Tuesday, she walks $\frac{1}{2}$ mile farther than she walked on Monday. How far did Sun walk on Tuesday?

   A $\frac{1}{3}$ mile

   B $\frac{3}{4}$ mile

   C $1\frac{1}{6}$ miles

   D $1\frac{1}{3}$ miles

Guided Instruction 1

When you add or subtract fractions, you need to pay close attention to the denominator of the fraction. You will first study how to add and subtract fractions with the same denominator.

$\frac{1}{8} + \frac{3}{8} = \square$

What is the **sum**?

Think About It

Add the fractions to find the sum. You can use fraction strips to show each fraction. Then, count how many to find the sum.

$$\boxed{\frac{1}{8}} + \boxed{\frac{1}{8}}\boxed{\frac{1}{8}}\boxed{\frac{1}{8}} = \boxed{\frac{1}{8}}\boxed{\frac{1}{8}}\boxed{\frac{1}{8}}\boxed{\frac{1}{8}}$$

$$\frac{1}{8} + \frac{3}{8} = \frac{4}{8}$$

Now, write the sum in **simplest form**.

$$\boxed{\frac{1}{8}}\boxed{\frac{1}{8}}\boxed{\frac{1}{8}}\boxed{\frac{1}{8}}$$

$$\boxed{\frac{1}{2}}$$

$$\frac{4}{8} = \frac{1}{2}$$

So, $\frac{1}{8} + \frac{3}{8} = \frac{1}{2}$.

Try This Strategy

Add the Numerators

If 2 fractions have the same **denominator,** add the **numerators** to find the sum. The denominator stays the same.

What is the sum of $\frac{1}{6}$ and $\frac{4}{6}$?

$\frac{1}{6} + \frac{4}{6} = \frac{5}{6}$

You can use the same strategy for subtraction.

Study the problem. Use the **Math Guide** for tips that can help you understand how to subtract fractions with common denominators.

 Math Guide

The fractions have the same denominator.	What is $\frac{7}{8} - \frac{5}{8}$?
Show $\frac{7}{8}$ using fraction strips.	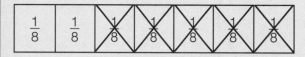
Cross out $\frac{5}{8}$ of the fraction strips.	
Count the left over fraction strips to find the **difference**. Write the difference in simplest form.	$\frac{2}{8} = \frac{1}{4}$ So, $\frac{7}{8} - \frac{5}{8} = \frac{1}{4}$.

Now, use what you already know and what you learned to **add and subtract fractions with the same denominators.**

Answer the questions on the next page.

Practice adding and subtracting fractions by solving the problems below.

EXAMPLE

What is $\frac{2}{5} - \frac{1}{5}$?

A $\frac{2}{5}$

B $\frac{3}{10}$

C $\frac{1}{5}$

D $\frac{1}{10}$

What do you need to find?

Find the difference by subtracting the fractions.

The denominators are the same, so you can subtract the numerators.

$$\frac{2}{5} - \frac{1}{5} = \frac{1}{5}$$

Now read each question. Circle the letter of the best answer. You may use fraction strips.

1. $\frac{7}{10} - \frac{5}{10} = \square$

What is the difference?

A $\frac{2}{5}$

B $\frac{1}{5}$

C $\frac{1}{10}$

D $\frac{2}{0}$

3. $\frac{3}{8} + \frac{3}{8} = \square$

What is the sum?

A $\frac{3}{4}$

B $\frac{2}{3}$

C $\frac{3}{8}$

D $\frac{3}{16}$

2. What is $\frac{2}{4} + \frac{1}{4}$?

A $\frac{1}{8}$

B $\frac{3}{8}$

C $\frac{1}{2}$

D $\frac{3}{4}$

4. What is $\frac{6}{9} - \frac{3}{9}$?

A $\frac{1}{9}$

B $\frac{1}{3}$

C $\frac{1}{2}$

D $\frac{3}{1}$

Happy Birthday, Fido!

Newport Beach, CA—Many dog owners buy their pets clothes, special treats, and soft beds. A new trend for dog owners is throwing a birthday party—for the dog!

Birthday parties, complete with party hats, cake, and guests (with their owners), are surprisingly common. There are even bakeries that will make dog-friendly birthday cakes.

There is one difference between dog birthdays and people birthdays. People celebrate birthdays on the day they were born. Most pet owners celebrate their dogs' birthdays on the day the dog came to live with the family.

Solve It

Imagine you work in a bakery making birthday treats for dogs. Show your work on a separate sheet of paper. Write your answer in simplest form.

1. A recipe for dog bones calls for $\frac{1}{4}$ cup water and $\frac{3}{4}$ cup chicken broth.
   How much more chicken broth than water is needed for the recipe? _____

2. A dog birthday cake has $\frac{1}{8}$ cup of corn meal and $\frac{5}{8}$ cup of flour.
   How much corn meal and flour is needed in all for the cake? _____

3. It takes a baker $\frac{1}{6}$ hour to prepare the birthday cake batter.
   It then takes $\frac{4}{6}$ hour to bake the cake in the oven.
   How long does it take to prepare the batter and bake the cake? _____

Ladder to Success

Review

You have learned how to add and subtract fractions.

Review the methods you can use to add and subtract fractions.

- You can use fraction strips to add and subtract fractions.
- You can use paper and pencil to add and subtract fractions.

Practice 1

Sam spent $\frac{3}{6}$ of an hour studying his spelling words. He then spent $\frac{5}{6}$ of an hour working on his science fair project. How much longer did he spend working on his science fair project than studying his spelling words?

What I Already Know	Sam spent $\frac{3}{6}$ of an hour studying his spelling words and $\frac{5}{6}$ of an hour working on his science fair project.
What I Need to Find Out	How much longer did Sam spend working on his science fair project than studying his spelling words?
What I Need to Do	Find $\frac{5}{6} - \frac{3}{6}$.

You can use fraction strips to solve the problem.

Cross out the fraction strips to show taking $\frac{3}{6}$ away from $\frac{5}{6}$.

$\frac{1}{6}$	$\frac{1}{6}$	$\frac{1}{6}$	$\frac{1}{6}$	$\frac{1}{6}$

Use the models to complete the number sentence: $\frac{5}{6} - \frac{3}{6} = \boxed{}$

How much longer did Sam spend working on his science fair project than studying his spelling words? Show your answer in simplest form. _____

1. What is $\frac{3}{9} + \frac{1}{9}$?

A $\frac{2}{18}$ C $\frac{4}{9}$

B $\frac{4}{18}$ D $\frac{5}{9}$

2. What is $\frac{3}{5} - \frac{1}{5}$?

A $\frac{2}{0}$ C $\frac{2}{10}$

B $\frac{2}{5}$ D $\frac{3}{25}$

Practice 2

At the Farmer's Market, Greta bought $\frac{3}{4}$ pound of green grapes and $\frac{2}{4}$ pound of red grapes. How many pounds of grapes did Greta buy in all?

What I Already Know	Greta bought $\frac{3}{4}$ pound of green grapes and $\frac{2}{4}$ pound of red grapes.
What I Need to Find Out	How many pounds of grapes did Greta buy in all?
What I Need to Do	Find $\frac{3}{4} + \frac{2}{4}$.

Since $\frac{3}{4}$ and $\frac{2}{4}$ have the same denominator, use paper and pencil to add the fractions.

Complete the problem.

$$\begin{array}{r} \frac{3}{4} \\ + \frac{2}{4} \\ \hline \end{array}$$

The sum is _____.

Use fraction strips to rewrite the fraction in simplest form.

$\frac{1}{4}$	$\frac{1}{4}$	$\frac{1}{4}$	$\frac{1}{4}$	$\frac{1}{4}$

1	$\frac{1}{4}$

$\frac{5}{4} = 1\frac{1}{4}$

What is the sum in simplest form? _____

How many pounds of grapes did Greta buy in all? _____

---

1. $\frac{7}{8} + \frac{2}{8} = \boxed{}$

What is the sum?

A $\frac{9}{16}$

B $\frac{8}{8}$

C $1\frac{1}{8}$

D $1\frac{9}{8}$

2. $\frac{8}{10} - \frac{4}{10} = \boxed{}$

What is the difference?

A $2\frac{4}{5}$

B $2\frac{2}{5}$

C $\frac{4}{5}$

D $\frac{2}{5}$

Practice 3

Lisa is using the recipe shown to make banana bread.

How many cups of flour will Lisa need in all to make the bread? Show your answer in simplest form.

Banana Bread	
2 cups mashed banana	$\frac{3}{4}$ cup oil
$\frac{1}{8}$ cup light brown sugar	2 eggs
$\frac{3}{8}$ cup dark brown sugar	$\frac{3}{8}$ teaspoon salt
$\frac{3}{4}$ cup white flour	$\frac{3}{4}$ teaspoon baking soda
$\frac{1}{4}$ cup wheat flour	$\frac{1}{8}$ teaspoon cinnamon

Reread the problem to see what you need to do.

You need to find out how much flour Lisa will need in all. This means you should add $\frac{3}{4}$ and $\frac{1}{4}$ to find the sum.

How can you add $\frac{3}{4}$ and $\frac{1}{4}$?

You can add the fractions using paper and pencil.

Complete the addition on your own.

$$\begin{array}{r} \frac{3}{4} \\ + \frac{1}{4} \\ \hline \end{array}$$

Write the sum in simplest form. _____

Explain how you wrote the sum in simplest form.

When the numerator and the denominator of a fraction are the same, the fraction is equal to 1.

_____

_____

How much flour will Lisa need to make the bread?

_____

1. How much more dark brown sugar does Lisa need than light brown sugar? Show your answer in simplest form.

_____

2. Lisa wants to make another recipe that uses $\frac{5}{8}$ cup of white flour and $\frac{4}{8}$ cup of wheat flour. How many cups of flour does Lisa need in all for the recipe? Show your answer in simplest form.

_____

Guided Instruction 2

You will build upon what you learned in Part 1 by learning to add and subtract fractions with different denominators.

What is $\frac{1}{3} + \frac{1}{4}$?

Think About It

The fractions have different denominators, so you can use the **least common denominator (LCD)** to solve this problem.

Find the LCD by listing some of the **multiples** of each denominator.

Multiples of 3: 3, 6, 9, (12), 15
Multiples of 4: 4, 8, (12), 16, 20
So, 12 is the least common multiple. 12 is the least common denominator.

Rename the fractions as **equivalent fractions** using the LCD.

$$\frac{1}{3} = \frac{1 \times 4}{3 \times 4} = \frac{4}{12}$$

$\frac{1}{3}$			
$\frac{1}{12}$	$\frac{1}{12}$	$\frac{1}{12}$	$\frac{1}{12}$

$$\frac{1}{4} = \frac{1 \times 3}{4 \times 3} = \frac{3}{12}$$

$\frac{1}{4}$		
$\frac{1}{12}$	$\frac{1}{12}$	$\frac{1}{12}$

Add the equivalent fractions to find the sum.

$$\frac{4}{12} + \frac{3}{12} = \frac{7}{12}$$

So, $\frac{1}{3} + \frac{1}{4} = \frac{7}{12}$.

Try This Strategy

Denominators as Multiples

What is $\frac{5}{6} - \frac{1}{2}$?

Six is a multiple of 2 and 6, so you only need to rename $\frac{1}{2}$ using 6 as the denominator.

$$\frac{1}{2} = \frac{1 \times 3}{2 \times 3} = \frac{3}{6}$$

Since $\frac{5}{6} - \frac{3}{6} = \frac{2}{6}$ or $\frac{1}{3}$ then, $\frac{5}{6} - \frac{1}{2} = \frac{1}{3}$.

Study the problem. Use the Math Guide for tips that can help you understand how to subtract fractions with different denominators.

 Math Guide

The fractions do not have the same denominators. They need to be renamed.	What is $\frac{1}{2} - \frac{1}{5}$?
The common denominator of 2 and 5 is 10.	$\frac{1}{2} = \frac{1 \times 5}{2 \times 5} = \frac{5}{10}$ $\frac{1}{5} = \frac{1 \times 2}{5 \times 2} = \frac{2}{10}$
Subtract the fractions.	$\frac{5}{10} - \frac{2}{10} = \frac{3}{10}$
Check that your answer is in simplest form.	So, $\frac{1}{2} - \frac{1}{5} = \frac{3}{10}$.

Now, use what you already know and what you learned to add and subtract fractions with different denominators.

Answer the questions on the next page.

Practice the Skill 2

Choose the correct answer. You may use fraction strips.

1. What is $\frac{1}{3} + \frac{1}{9}$?

   A $\frac{2}{9}$

   B $\frac{1}{6}$

   C $\frac{4}{9}$

   D $\frac{2}{3}$

2. $\frac{3}{4} - \frac{2}{8} = \boxed{}$

   What is the difference?

   A $\frac{1}{2}$

   B $\frac{1}{4}$

   C $\frac{1}{6}$

   D $\frac{1}{8}$

3. $\frac{2}{3} + \frac{2}{5} = \boxed{}$

   What is the sum?

   A $1\frac{4}{15}$

   B $1\frac{1}{15}$

   C $\frac{1}{2}$

   D $\frac{1}{4}$

4. What is $\frac{7}{8} - \frac{3}{4}$?

   A $\frac{1}{8}$

   B $\frac{1}{6}$

   C $\frac{1}{2}$

   D $\frac{2}{3}$

5. The soccer team warms up for $\frac{1}{2}$ of an hour in all. They do drills for $\frac{1}{3}$ of an hour and the rest of the warm-up is spent stretching. How much time does the team spend stretching?

   A $\frac{2}{5}$ of an hour

   B $\frac{1}{5}$ of an hour

   C $\frac{2}{6}$ of an hour

   D $\frac{1}{6}$ of an hour

6. Laurie buys $\frac{1}{4}$ pound of Swiss cheese and $\frac{2}{3}$ pound of American cheese. How much cheese does Laurie buy in all?

   A $\frac{3}{7}$ pound

   B $\frac{7}{12}$ pound

   C $\frac{11}{12}$ pound

   D 1 pound

Unusual Friends

San Diego, CA—Koza and Cairo are not typical friends. Koza is a lion cub, and Cairo is a puppy. They live together at the San Diego Zoo.

Koza was the only lion cub at the zoo. Zookeepers were worried that he would not learn how to live with other lions. Since there were no lion cubs, zookeepers searched for another playmate for Koza.

Cairo was left by his owners and needed a new home. The zookeepers thought that he would be a good playmate for Koza. At first, Koza was shy around Cairo, but over time he started to play with the puppy. Koza and Cairo now play happily together.

Solve It

Imagine that you visited the zoo to see Koza and Cairo as you answer the questions. Show your work on a separate sheet of paper.

1. The zookeeper gives Koza $\frac{1}{4}$ pound of food for his first feeding and $\frac{1}{3}$ pound of food for his second feeding. How much food does Koza eat during his first two feedings?

   _____

2. Koza and Cairo play with a pull toy for $\frac{1}{2}$ of an hour. They then play with another toy for $\frac{1}{4}$ of an hour. How much time do Koza and Cairo spend playing with toys?

   _____

Show What You Learned

Now that you have practiced adding and subtracting fractions, take this quiz to show what you learned. Choose the letter of the correct answer for each problem.

1. $\frac{1}{6} + \frac{4}{6} = \square$

What is the sum?

A $\frac{1}{3}$

B $\frac{5}{12}$

C $\frac{1}{2}$

D $\frac{5}{6}$

2. What is $\frac{5}{9} - \frac{2}{9}$?

A $\frac{1}{6}$

B $\frac{1}{4}$

C $\frac{1}{3}$

D $\frac{3}{0}$

3. $\frac{7}{8} - \frac{1}{8} = \square$

Which fraction completes the number sentence?

A 1

B $\frac{3}{4}$

C $\frac{2}{3}$

D $\frac{6}{0}$

4. $\frac{5}{6} + \frac{4}{6} = \square$

What is the sum?

A $1\frac{1}{2}$

B $1\frac{1}{3}$

C $\frac{3}{4}$

D $\frac{1}{2}$

5. Jessica spends $\frac{3}{8}$ of an hour practicing piano. She then spends $\frac{5}{8}$ of an hour doing her homework. How much time does Jessica spend practicing piano and doing her homework?

A $\frac{1}{4}$ hour

B $\frac{1}{2}$ hour

C $\frac{7}{8}$ hour

D 1 hour

6. Miguel rides his bike $\frac{5}{6}$ of a mile to school. So far today, he has biked $\frac{2}{6}$ of a mile. How much farther does he have to ride to get to school?

A $\frac{1}{8}$ mile

B $\frac{1}{2}$ mile

C $1\frac{1}{6}$ miles

D $\frac{3}{0}$ mile

7. $\frac{2}{3} - \frac{1}{6} = \square$

   What is the difference?

   A $\frac{5}{6}$

   B $\frac{3}{4}$

   C $\frac{1}{2}$

   D $\frac{1}{3}$

8. What is $\frac{1}{4} + \frac{3}{8}$?

   A $\frac{5}{8}$

   B $\frac{2}{3}$

   C $\frac{3}{4}$

   D 1

9. $\frac{5}{6} - \frac{2}{3} = \square$

   Which fraction completes the number sentence?

   A $\frac{1}{6}$

   B $\frac{1}{3}$

   C $\frac{5}{6}$

   D $\frac{3}{3}$

10. $\frac{1}{3} + \frac{3}{4} = \square$

    What is the sum?

    A $\frac{1}{12}$

    B $\frac{4}{7}$

    C $1\frac{1}{12}$

    D $1\frac{1}{8}$

11. Ross runs $\frac{5}{8}$ of a mile on Monday. He runs $\frac{1}{4}$ of a mile farther on Tuesday. How far does Ross run on Tuesday?

    A $\frac{11}{12}$ of a mile

    B $\frac{7}{8}$ of a mile

    C $\frac{5}{6}$ of a mile

    D $\frac{3}{8}$ of a mile

Show your work on a separate sheet of paper.

12. Explain the steps you use to solve the problem below and show the answer in simplest form.

    Cory buys $\frac{3}{4}$ pound of macaroni salad and $\frac{1}{2}$ pound of egg salad at the deli. How many pounds of macaroni salad and egg salad does Cory buy in all?

Show What You Know

Before you begin this lesson on perimeter and area, answer these questions. Choose the letter of the correct answer for each problem.

1. What is the perimeter of the square?

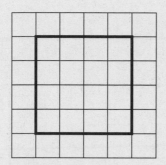

A 4 units

B 8 units

C 12 units

D 16 units

2. What is the area of the rectangle?

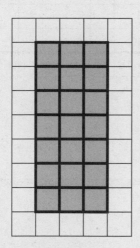

A 10 square units

B 13 square units

C 21 square units

D 26 square units

3. What is the perimeter of the rectangle?

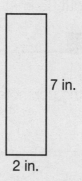

7 in.

2 in.

A 18 in.

B 16 in.

C 14 in.

D 9 in.

4. What is the area of the rectangle?

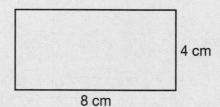

4 cm

8 cm

A 64 cm^2

B 32 cm^2

C 24 cm^2

D 12 cm^2

When you find **perimeter**, you find the distance around a figure. When you find **area**, you find the amount of surface enclosed in a closed figure. In Part 1, you will learn more about perimeter and area.

Here's How

What is the perimeter of this **rectangle**?

Think About It

You can count around the outside of the figure to find the perimeter.

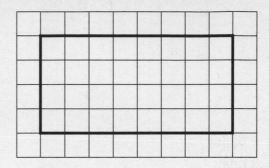

Count the number of units around the outside of the rectangle. Be sure to start and stop in the same spot.

There are 24 units around the rectangle, so the perimeter of the rectangle is 24 units.

Try This Strategy

Add the Lengths of the Sides

What is the perimeter of the rectangle?

You can add the lengths of the **sides** to find the perimeter.

perimeter = 5 cm + 3 cm + 5 cm + 3 cm
perimeter = 16 cm

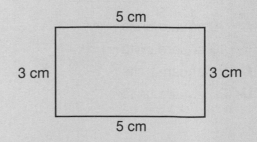

Duplicating any part of this book is prohibited by law.

Study the problem. Use the **Math Guide** for tips that can help you understand how to find the area of a rectangle.

 Math Guide

Notice the question asks you to find the *area*.	What is the area of a rectangle that is 9 cm long and 4 cm wide?
Be sure the rectangle is 9 by 4 on the grid.	You can draw the rectangle on a sheet of grid paper. 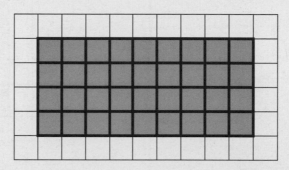
Count *only* the shaded squares inside the grid.	Count the number of shaded squares inside the rectangle to find the area of the rectangle.
Area is always measured in square units (or units^2).	There are 36 shaded squares inside the rectangle, so the area of the rectangle is 36 square centimeters (or cm^2).

Now, use what you already know and what you learned to find **perimeter and area of figures**.

Answer the questions on the next page.

Practice the Skill 1

Practice finding perimeter and area by solving the problems below.

EXAMPLE

What is the area of a square with sides that are 5 in. long?

A 5 in.²

B 10 in.²

C 20 in.²

D 25 in.²

What do you need to find?

Find the area by drawing a **square** on grid paper.

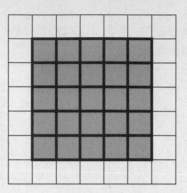

Now, read each question. Circle the letter of the correct answer.

1. What is the perimeter of the square?

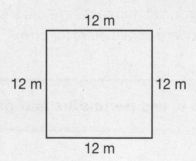

12 m

12 m   12 m

12 m

A 24 m

B 36 m

C 48 m

D 144 m

2. What is the area of a rectangle with these measurements?

length = 11 cm
width = 3 cm

A 33 cm²

B 30 cm²

C 28 cm²

D 14 cm²

WATCHING EAGLES

Southbury, CT—During the winter, northern bald eagles live near Shepaug Dam. The eagles fly from Canada to New England for the winter. But the eagles usually eat fresh fish. So, when rivers and ponds freeze, the eagles have a hard time finding food.

But the pool at the bottom of the Shepaug Dam does not freeze. Moving water keeps it from freezing and pushes the fish in the pool to the surface. Eagles can then fly down and eat fresh fish!

The Shepaug Dam has a viewing area for people to watch the eagles. About 11 eagles eat at the dam every day.

Solve It

Imagine you observe the eagles at the Shepaug Dam as you answer the questions. Show your work on a separate sheet of paper.

Eagles were seen in a rectangular area of land like the one shown.

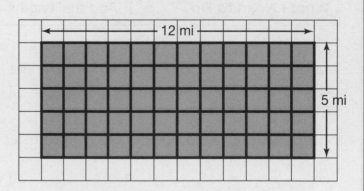

12 mi

5 mi

1. What is the perimeter of the land where the eagles were seen?

_____

2. What is the area of the land where the eagles were seen?

_____

Ladder to Success

Review

You have learned how to find the perimeter and area of squares and rectangles.

Review the methods you can use to find perimeter and area.

- Count squares or add the lengths of the sides to find the perimeter of a figure.
- Count squares to find the area of a figure.

Practice 1

What is the perimeter of the rectangle?

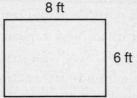

8 ft

6 ft

What I Already Know	One side of the rectangle is 8 ft long. Another side of the rectangle is 6 ft long.
What I Need to Find Out	What is the perimeter of the rectangle?
What I Need to Do	Add the lengths of the sides to find the perimeter.

The drawing has only 2 sides of the rectangle labeled. But, since opposite sides of a rectangle are the same length, you can find the lengths of the other 2 sides.

Add the lengths of the sides to find the perimeter.

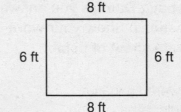

8 ft

6 ft   6 ft

8 ft

_____ ft + _____ ft + _____ ft + _____ ft = _____ ft

The perimeter of the rectangle is _____ feet.

---

1. What is the perimeter of the square?

A 12 in.
B 24 in.
C 36 in.
D 60 in.

6 in.

2. What is the perimeter of the rectangle?

A 84 ft
B 42 ft
C 38 ft
D 19 ft

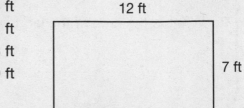

12 ft

7 ft

Practice 2

Use a centimeter ruler to find the perimeter of the rectangle.

To find the perimeter, you need to measure the length and width of the rectangle using a centimeter ruler.

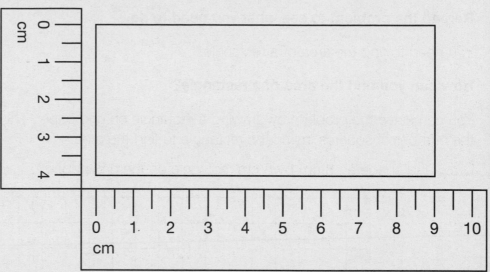

The length of the rectangle is _____ cm.

The width of the rectangle is _____ cm.

Add the lengths of the sides to find the perimeter.

_____ cm + _____ cm + _____ cm + _____ cm = _____ cm

The perimeter of the rectangle is _____ cm.

---

1. What is the perimeter of the square?
   Use an *inch ruler* to measure.

   A 2 inches

   B 4 inches

   C 8 inches

   D 12 inches

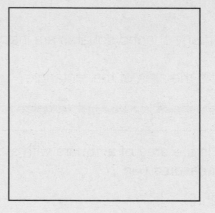

Practice 3

What is the area of a rectangle that is 8 cm long and 5 cm wide?

Reread the problem to see what you need to do.

You need to find the area of a rectangle.

How can you find the area of a rectangle?

You can solve the problem by drawing a rectangle on grid paper. Then, you can count the number of squares inside the rectangle to find the area.

Draw and shade an 8 cm by 5 cm rectangle on the grid paper.

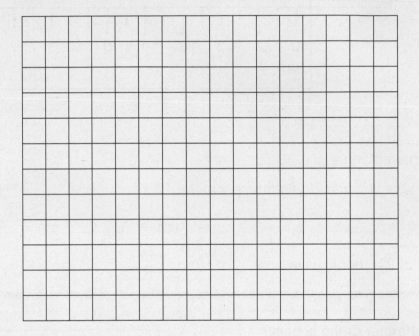

How many shaded squares are inside the rectangle? _____

What is the area of the rectangle? _____

---

1. What is the area of a square with a side that measures 6 in.?

   A 12 in.²

   B 24 in.²

   C 32 in.²

   D 36 in.²

2. What is the area of a rectangle that is 9 ft long and 2 ft wide?

   A 11 ft²

   B 18 ft²

   C 22 ft²

   D 36 ft²

In Part 2, you will learn and apply **formulas** for finding perimeter and area.

Here's How

What is the perimeter of the rectangle shown below?

Think About It

Since opposite sides of a rectangle are the same length, the perimeter is equal to 2 times the length plus 2 times the width.

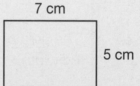

7 cm

5 cm

Perimeter = (2 × length) + (2 × width)

$P = 2l + 2w$

$P = (2 × 7) + (2 × 5)$

$P = 14 + 10$

$P = 24$ cm

So, the perimeter of the rectangle is 24 cm.

Try This Strategy

Perimeter of a Square

Since all 4 sides of a square are the same length, the perimeter is equal to 4 times the length of a side.

What is the perimeter of the square?

Perimeter = 4 × length of one side

$P = 4s$

$P = 4 × 6$

$P = 24$ in.

6 in.

The perimeter of the square is 24 in.

Study the problem. Use the **Math Guide** for tips that can help you understand the formula for area of a rectangle.

 Math Guide

Carefully read the measures of the **length** and **width** of the rectangle.	What is the area of the rectangle? 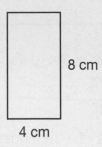 8 cm 4 cm
The formula for area uses multiplication.	The area of a rectangle is found by multiplying length by width.
You can also write the formula $A = lw$.	Area = length × width $A = l \times w$ $A = 8 \text{ cm} \times 4 \text{ cm}$ $A = 32$ square centimeters (cm²)
Area is always measured in square units (units²).	So, the area of the rectangle is 32 cm².

Now, use what you already know and what you learned to **find the perimeter and area of squares and rectangles.**

Answer the questions on the next page.

Practice the Skill 2

Choose the correct answer.

1. What is the perimeter of the square?

9 m

A 18 m

B 36 m

C 72 m

D 81 m

2. What is the perimeter of the figure?

7 ft

3 ft

A 10 feet

B 13 feet

C 17 feet

D 20 feet

3. What is the area of the rectangle?

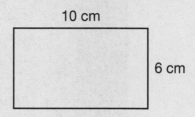

10 cm

6 cm

A 16 cm^2

B 32 cm^2

C 60 cm^2

D 66 cm^2

4. Which formula can you use to find the area of the figure?

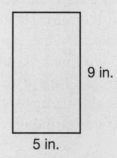

9 in.

5 in.

A $A = lw$

B $A = 2l + 2w$

C $A = 4s$

D $A = s^2$

A Papyrus Treasure

Turin, Italy—An ancient Greek papyrus was put together from over 50 small pieces. Papyrus was a material used by the ancient Greeks and Romans. They wrote and drew on the material. This papyrus is amazing because it was used at different times by different people. Part of the papyrus shows the world's oldest map. Another part of the papyrus has stories and drawings.

The papyrus was first used over 2,000 years ago by a map maker and storyteller. Then, the papyrus ended up in a painter's studio where students used blank spots to practice drawing heads, feet, and hands. The papyrus was then used to wrap a mummy. It stayed in the ground for 1,800 years until it was discovered and slowly pieced back together!

Solve It

Imagine the drawing shown is from the papyrus. Show your work on a separate sheet of paper.

8 in.

12 in.

1. What is the perimeter of the drawing?

_____

2. What is the area of the drawing?

_____

Show What You Learned

Now that you have practiced finding perimeter and area, take this quiz to show what you learned. Choose the letter of the correct answer for each problem.

Use the diagram below for problems 1 and 2.

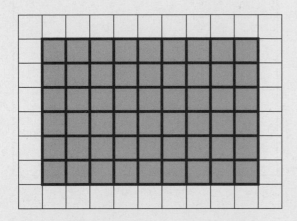

1. What is the perimeter of the rectangle?

   A 15 units

   B 30 units

   C 54 units

   D 96 units

2. What is the area of the rectangle?

   A 54 square units

   B 45 square units

   C 30 square units

   D 15 square units

Use the diagram below for problems 3 and 4.

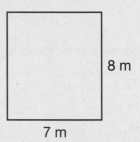

8 m

7 m

3. Which formula can you use to find the perimeter of the figure?

   A $P = lw$

   B $P = 4s$

   C $P = s^2$

   D $P = 2l + 2w$

4. What is the area of the figure?

   A 15 m^2

   B 30 m^2

   C 56 m^2

   D 112 m^2

Use the diagram below for problems 5 and 6.

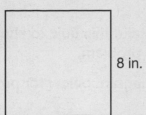

8 in.

5. What is the perimeter of the square?

   A 12 in.

   B 16 in.

   C 32 in.

   D 64 in.

6. What is the area of the square?

   A 80 in.^{2}

   B 64 in.^{2}

   C 40 in.^{2}

   D 32 in.^{2}

7. What is the area of this figure?

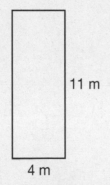

11 m

4 m

   A 44 m^2

   B 30 m^2

   C 22 m^2

   D 15 m^2

Show your work on a separate sheet of paper.

8. Use a centimeter ruler to measure the length and width of the rectangle. Then, use your measurements to find the perimeter and area of the rectangle.

Show What You Know

Before you begin this lesson on angles and triangles, answer these questions. Choose the letter of the correct answer for each problem.

1. Which type of angle is shown?

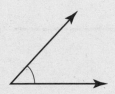

  A right angle
  B acute angle
  C obtuse angle
  D scalene angle

2. Which shows a right angle?

  A

  B

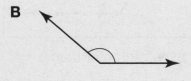

  C

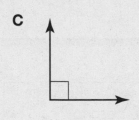

  D

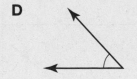

3. Which shows an obtuse triangle?

  A

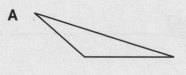

  B

  C

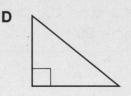

  D

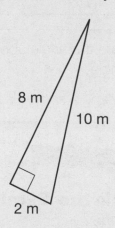

4. How can you best classify the triangle?

8 m
10 m
2 m

  A acute, isosceles triangle
  B acute, equilateral triangle
  C right, isosceles triangle
  D right, scalene triangle

An **angle** is a figure formed by 2 **rays** that share an **endpoint**. In Part 1, you will learn how to classify angles and then apply this skill to classify **triangles**.

Here's How

How can you classify the angle?

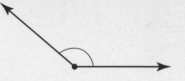

Think About It

You can classify the angle based on its opening.

A **right angle** forms a square corner and measures exactly 90°.	An **acute angle** is less than a right angle.	An **obtuse angle** is greater than a right angle.

Compare the angle above to the angles in the chart. The angle is greater than a right angle.

So, the angle shown is an obtuse angle.

Try This Strategy

Check the Symbols

Notice the symbols used on angles. The symbols can help you classify angles.

A square corner symbol shows that the angle is a right angle.	An arc shows the angle that you need to classify.

Study the problem. Use the **Math Guide** for tips that can help you understand how to classify a triangle using angles.

Math Guide

What type of triangle is shown below?

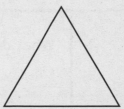

You can classify the triangle based on its angles.

Compare each angle of the triangle to a right angle.

Carefully read the definitions of each type of triangle.

A **right triangle** has one right angle.	An **acute triangle** has three acute angles.	An **obtuse triangle** has one obuse angle.

Compare the triangle above to the triangles in the chart.

The triangle shown has 3 acute angles.

The triangle shown is an acute triangle.

Now use what you already know and what you learned to **classify angles and triangles.**

Answer the questions on the next page.

Practice classifying angles and triangles by solving the problems below.

EXAMPLE

Which type of triangle is shown?

A acute triangle

B obtuse triangle

C right triangle

D equal triangle

What do you need to do?

Classify the triangle by looking at its angles.

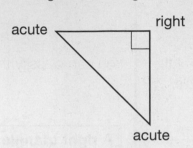

Now, read each question. Circle the letter of the correct answer.

1. Which type of angle is shown?

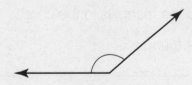

A obtuse angle

B right angle

C acute angle

D equilateral angle

2. How can you classify the triangle?

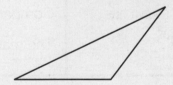

A acute triangle

B obtuse triangle

C right triangle

D parallel triangle

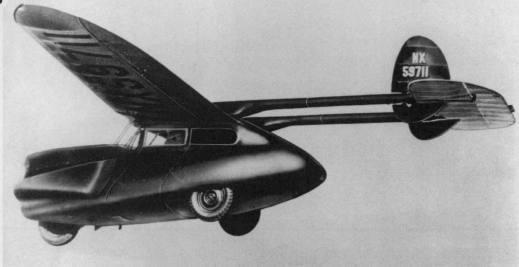

Flying Cars

Cambridge, MA—Students at the Massachusetts Institute of Technology (MIT) have made plans for a flying car. Flying cars have long been a part of made-up stories. The students want to make flying cars part of real life.

Since 1917, people have been trying to make a flying car, but they have always run into the same problem. A flying car has never been as good as either a car or a plane.

The student team at MIT thinks that they have solved the problem. They have a plan that uses new materials. They think that the materials will make the difference in their flying car. Maybe by the time you start to drive, you will learn to drive a flying car!

Solve It

The drawing shows a plan for a flying car. Use the drawing to answer the questions.

1. What type of angle does the tip of the airplane wing have? _____

2. How would you classify the triangle shape of the airplane window? _____

Ladder to Success

Review

You have learned how to classify angles and triangles.

Review the methods you can use to classify angles and triangles.

- Compare angles to find if they are equal to, less than, or greater than a right angle.
- Identify the angles of a triangle to classify it as acute, obtuse, or right.

Practice 1

Jenna drew the angle shown. Did she draw a right angle, an acute angle, or an obtuse angle?

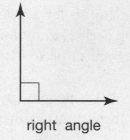

Reread the problem to see what you need to do.
You need to classify Jenna's angle as a right angle, an acute angle, or an obtuse angle.

How can you classify Jenna's angle?
You can compare Jenna's angle to a right angle to classify it.

An acute angle will be
less than a right angle.
An obtuse angle will be
greater than a right angle.

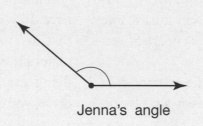

Jenna's angle   right angle

How can you classify Jenna's angle? _____

How can you tell? _____

_____

---

1. Which type of angle is greater than a right angle?

   A acute angle

   B equal angle

   C obtuse angle

   D scalene angle

2. Which completes the statement?

   An acute angle _____.

   A is greater than a right angle

   B is less than a right angle

   C is the same size as a right angle

   D forms a square corner

Practice 2

Ryan drew the angles shown. What type of angles did he draw?

Reread the problem to see what you need to do.
You need to classify Ryan's angles.

How can you classify Ryan's angles?
You can compare each one of the angles to a right angle to classify it.

Classify each angle.

Ryan's Angles

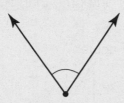 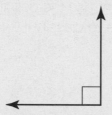 

_____   _____   _____

How did you know how to classify the second angle?

_____

_____

---

1. Which type of angle is shown?

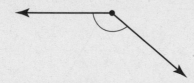

    A acute angle
    B right angle
    C obtuse angle
    D scalene angle

2. Which type of angle is shown?

    A acute angle
    B equal angle
    C obtuse angle
    D right angle

Practice 3

How can you classify the triangle shown using its angles?

Reread the problem to see what you need to do.
You need to classify the triangle using its angles.

How can you classify the triangle?
Identify the angles in the triangle. Then, use the definitions of an acute triangle, an obtuse triangle, and a right triangle to classify it.

Compare each angle of the triangle
to a right angle to classify it.

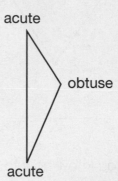

What type of triangle is shown? _____

How can you tell?

_____

_____

---

1. Which type of triangle is shown?

   A right triangle

   B acute triangle

   C obtuse triangle

   D equilateral triangle

2. Which type of triangle is shown?

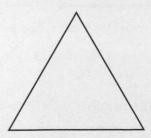

   A right triangle

   B acute triangle

   C obtuse triangle

   D scalene triangle

In Part 2, you will learn to classify triangles using angles and **sides**.

How can you classify the triangle shown by its sides?

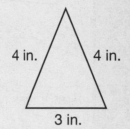

4 in.   4 in.

3 in.

Think About It

You can classify the triangle based on its sides.

An **isosceles triangle** has at least two sides or angles that are equal.	An **equilateral triangle** has three sides and angles that are equal.	A **scalene triangle** has no sides or angles that are equal.
3 m 3 m 2 m	2 m 2 m 2 m	2 m 3 m 4 m

Compare the triangle shown to the triangles in the chart. The triangle has 2 sides that are equal.

The triangle shown is an isosceles triangle.

Length Symbols

Tic marks on the sides of triangles indicate the length of the sides.

Sides with the same number of tic marks are the same length.

2 equal sides

3 equal sides

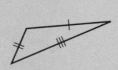

No equal sides

Study the problem. Use the Math Guide for tips that can help you understand how to classify a triangle by its sides *and* angles.

**Math
Guide**

Classify the triangle using both its sides and its angles.

Classify the triangle in as many ways as possible.

The triangle has 1 obtuse angle.

First, classify the triangle by its angles.

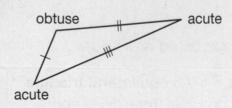

The triangle is obtuse.

The 3 sides are all different lengths.

Then, classify the triangle by its sides.
Notice that the tic marks show the sides are all different lengths.
The triangle is scalene.

So, the triangle is obtuse and scalene.

Now, use what you already know and what you learned to classify triangles.

**Answer the questions
on the next page.**

Choose the correct answer.

1. Which shows an equilateral triangle?

A
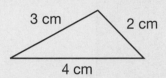
3 cm 2 cm 4 cm

B
2 cm 2 cm 1 cm

C
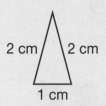
2 cm 2 cm 2 cm

D
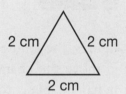
3 cm 1 cm 3 cm

2. What type of triangle is shown?

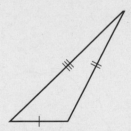

  A scalene triangle
  B isosceles triangle
  C acute triangle
  D equilateral triangle

3. How can you best classify the triangle?

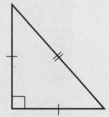

  A right, scalene triangle
  B right, isosceles triangle
  C acute, equilateral triangle
  D acute, isosceles triangle

4. Which shows a right, isosceles triangle?

A

B

C

D

MAKING MOVIES

Cannes, France—*Wallace and Gromit* and *Chicken Run* are both stop-motion films. They were made using clay figures that were posed for every single shot. It was a long and difficult job—but the movies that were made were terrific to watch.

The same studio that made those movies faced a new challenge to make *Flushed Away*.

Instead of using clay figures, the studio used computers to draw and move the characters. The studio says that it has no plans to stop using stop-motion in other films, but it is pleased to also have computers to use. The studio can now use computers or stop-motion, whichever one is better for the story it wants to tell.

Solve It

Some clay figures have features that are shaped like triangles.
Use the clay figure to answer the questions.

1. Write two ways you can classify the clay figure's triangle eyes.

   _____

2. Write two ways you can classify the clay figure's triangle mouth.

   _____

Show What You Learned

Now that you have practiced classifying angles and triangles, take this quiz to show what you learned. Choose the letter of the correct answer for each problem.

1. Which shows an obtuse angle?

A

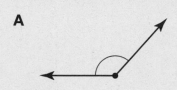

B

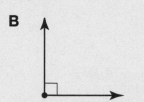

C

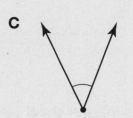

D

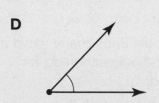

2. What type of triangle is shown?

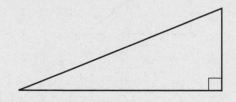

A acute triangle

B obtuse triangle

C right triangle

D equilateral triangle

3. Which shows an isosceles triangle?

A

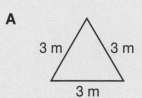
3 m   3 m
3 m

B

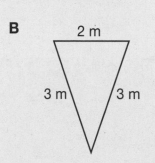
2 m
3 m   3 m

C

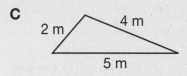
2 m   4 m
5 m

D

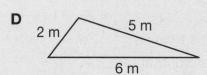
2 m   5 m
6 m

4. Hannah draws an angle that is less than a right angle. Which type of angle did she draw?

A scalene angle

B equal angle

C obtuse angle

D acute angle

5. Which shows a right angle?

A

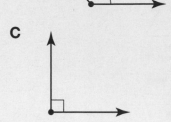

B

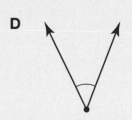

C

D

6. Marcus draws a triangle with 3 sides that are equal. Which type of triangle did he draw?

A scalene triangle

B equilateral triangle

C isosceles triangle

D balanced triangle

7. Which shows a right, scalene triangle?

A

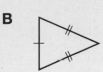

B

C

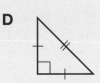

D

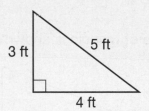

Show your work on a separate sheet of paper.

8. Classify the triangle in as many ways as possible. Explain your reasoning for each classification.

3 ft   5 ft   4 ft

Show What You Know

Before you begin this lesson on function rules and tables, answer these questions. Choose the letter of the correct answer for each problem.

1. Which number is missing from the function table?

Number of Cartons	1	2	3	4	5
Number of Juice Boxes	3	6	☐	12	15

- **A** 7
- **B** 9
- **C** 10
- **D** 11

2. Which equation represents the statement?

A bean seedling is 3 times as tall as another seedling (s). How tall is the bean seedling (t)?

- **A** $t = 3s$
- **B** $t = s + 3$
- **C** $t = s \div 3$
- **D** $t = s - 3$

Use the function table for problems 3 and 4.

a	b
8	2
10	4
☐	6
14	8
16	10

3. Which number is missing from the function table?

- **A** 7
- **B** 10
- **C** 12
- **D** 13

4. Which equation is shown in the function table?

- **A** $b = 4a$
- **B** $b = a + 4$
- **C** $b = a \div 4$
- **D** $b = a - 6$

You can represent relationships using words, tables, and equations. In Part 1, you will learn how to show relationships using function tables and words.

What number is missing from the table?

Think About It

This is a **function table**. It shows the relationship between 2 quantities.

Number of Children	1	2	3	4	5
Number of Gloves	2	4	☐	8	10

You can use a **rule** to solve the problem.

Look at each pair of numbers in the table to find the rule. The number of gloves is always *twice* the number of children.

So, the rule is *multiply the number of children by 2 to find the number of gloves.*

Number of children   × 2 =   Number of gloves
↓   ↓   ↓
3   × 2 =   6

So, the missing number in the table is 6.

Use a Pattern

You can also complete a function table using a **pattern**.

The growth of the plant increases by 3 cm each week, so the missing growth number is 15.

3, 6, 9, 12, <u>15</u>

Week	1	2	3	4	5
Growth of Plant (cm)	3	6	9	12	☐

Study the problem. Use the **Math Guide** for tips that can help you understand how to make a function table to show a relationship.

Math Guide

The cost depends on the number of people, so this is a function.

Look for words that give clues about the rule to use in your function table.

It costs $4 per person to attend the school fair. How much does it cost if 2 people go? 4 people? 5 people?

Since cost depends on the number of people who go to the fair, you can make a function table to solve this problem.

Number of People	Total Cost
1	$4
2	$8
3	$12
4	$16
5	$20

The rule is: *The cost is equal to $4 multiplied by the number of people*

You could extend the function table to find the cost for more than 5 people.

You can use the information in the function table to solve the problem.

If 2 people go to the school fair, then it will cost $8.

If 4 people go to the school fair, then it will cost $16.

If 5 people go to the school fair, then it will cost $20.

Now, use what you already know and what you learned to solve problems using **function rules and tables**.

Answer the questions on the next page.

Practice the Skill 1

Practice solving equations by solving the problems below.

EXAMPLE

Which number is missing from the function table?

A   8

B   10

C   16

D   18

What do you need to find?

Find a rule to identify the missing number.

Week	Growth (in cm)
1	4
2	8
3	12
4	☐
5	20

The growth equals the number of weeks multiplied by 4.

Now, read each question. Circle the letter of the correct answer.

1. Which number is missing from the function table?

Number of Adults	Number of Students
1	3
2	4
3	☐
4	6
5	7

A   4

B   5

C   8

D   9

2. Which number is missing from the function table?

Number of Boxes	Number of Snack Bars
1	2
2	4
3	6
4	☐
5	10

A   8

B   9

C   10

D   11

Toy Robots

New York, NY—Over the past few years, toy sales have gone down. Children want electronics instead of toys. Now, toy makers are building new high-tech toys.

One new toy is a dinosaur robot. The robot has 7 computers. The computers help it move. They also help the robot react to things around it. If the robot is walking on a table and gets close to the edge, it will turn back around. The robot will cry and move like it is scared!

Toy makers hope that children of all ages will enjoy these new electronic toys.

Solve It

Make a function table to answer each question. Show your work on a separate sheet of paper.

1. One dinosaur robot has 7 computers in it. How many computers will 4 dinosaur robots have?

2. The head of the dinosaur robot has 3 motors in it. How many motors will 5 dinosaur robots have?

Ladder to Success

Review

You have learned how to find missing numbers in function tables and make function tables.

Review the ways you can use function tables.

- Use a rule to find a missing number in a function table.
- Use a pattern to find a missing number in a function table.

Practice 1

What number is missing from the table?

Reread the problem to see what you need to do.
You need to find a missing number from a function table.

How can you find the missing number?
You can use a rule to find the missing number.

Look at each pair of numbers shown in the table to find a rule. Write the number that completes each statement.

$3 \times$ _____ $= 12$ $5 \times$ _____ $= 20$

$9 \times$ _____ $= 36$ $15 \times$ _____ $= 60$

Write the number that completes the rule.

The number of marbles is equal to the number of cups times _____.

What number is missing from the table? _____

Number Cups	Number of Marbles
3	12
5	20
9	36
11	☐
15	60

Notice that the numbers in each column do **not** follow a pattern. You need to use a rule.

Use the function table to solve problems 1 and 2.

Time (min)	Distance (mi)
2	1
12	6
18	9
22	11
26	☐

1. What is the rule for the function table?

   A The distance is equal to the time multiplied by 2.

   B The distance is equal to the time plus 6.

   C The distance is equal to the time minus 11.

   D The distance is equal to the time divided by 2.

2. What is the missing number from the table?

   A 12   **B** 13   **C** 16   **D** 20

Practice 2

The chart shows the total amount of rainfall that occurs during a steady rain. What number is missing from the table?

Time (hours)	Rainfall (mm)
2	6
☐	12
6	18
8	24
10	30

Notice that the missing number is in the *first* column of the chart.

Reread the problem to see what you need to do.
You need to find a missing number from a function table.

How can you find the missing number?
You can use patterns or use a rule to find the missing number.

Use a Pattern	Use a Rule
The given times are: 2, ?, 6, 8, 10 From the given times, you can tell each time is 2 hours greater than the previous time. Complete the pattern and statement. 2, _____, 6, 8, 10 The missing number is _____.	Compare each given pair of numbers to write a rule. The number of hours is equal to the rainfall divided by _____. Complete the number sentence and statement. 12 ÷ _____ = _____ The missing number is _____.

Number of Vans	1	3	☐	7	9
Number of Passengers	7	21	35	49	63

Practice 3

Paul adds weights to a spring that is 3 inches long. Each time he adds a weight, the spring stretches 2 inches. How long will the spring be if Paul adds 4 weights?

What I Already Know	The spring is 3 inches long. It stretches 2 inches with each weight attached to it.
What I Need to Find Out	How long will the spring be with 4 weights?
What I Need to Do	Find the length of the spring.

Since the length of the spring depends on the number of weights, the relationship is a function. You can use a function table.

Number of Weights	0	1	2	3	4	5
Length of Spring (in.)	3	5	7	☐	☐	☐

Use the function table to solve the problem.

How long will the spring be if Paul adds 4 weights?

_____

Use the function table above to solve problems 1 and 2.

1. How long will the spring be if Paul adds 3 weights?

   A 8 inches
   B 9 inches
   C 10 inches
   D 12 inches

2. The spring is 13 inches long. How many weights did Paul add to the spring?

   A 5 weights
   B 4 weights
   C 3 weights
   D 2 weights

You will build upon what you have learned in Part 1 as you learn to write and use **equations** with function tables.

Here's How

Write an equation for this situation:

A plant starts as a seed and grows 4 cm per week. What is the height of the plant after a certain number of weeks?

Think About It

An equation is a mathematical statement with an equal sign.

Use **variables** in an equation to stand for unknown numbers.

Let h stand for the height of the plant.
Let w stand for the number of weeks.

Write the situation as a rule and then write the rule as an equation.

The height of a plant is equal to 4 times the number of weeks.

h = 4 × w

So, the equation is $h = 4 \times w$, or $h = 4w$.

Try This Strategy

Solve the Equation

How tall is the plant from the problem after 7 weeks?

You can solve this problem by substituting 7 for w in the equation.

$h = 4w$
$h = 4 \times 7$
$h = 28$ cm

Study the problem. Use the **Math Guide** for tips that can help you understand how to connect equations and function tables.

 Math Guide

Math Guide tips	Problem
The cost depends on the number of people, so this is a function.	A ticket to the museum costs $3. Write an equation you can use to find the cost for a group of people to go to the museum. Then, make a table of values for the equation for 1 to 6 people.
Use letters that represent what the variables stand for. This makes the meaning of the equation easier to understand.	Decide the variables you want to use for your equation. c = total cost to go to the museum p = number of people
Look for words that give clues about the operations to use in your equation.	Translate the words into an **expression**. Total cost equals $3 *times* the number of people: $c = \$3p$
Substitute values in the equation to complete the function table.	Then, make a table showing the values.

p	1	2	3	4	5	6
c	$3	$6	$9	$12	$15	$18

Now, use what you already know and what you learned to solve **function and equation problems**.

Answer the questions on the next page.

Choose the correct answer.

1. Which equation represents the statement?

   James is 5 years younger than his older sister. How old is James?

   A $j = s + 5$

   B $j = s - 5$

   C $j = s \div 5$

   D $j = s \times 5$

2. The equation below is used to find the number of bricks (b) used to build the rows of a wall (r).

   $b = 8r$

   How many bricks are needed to build seven rows of the wall?

   A 56 bricks

   B 49 bricks

   C 35 bricks

   D 15 bricks

3. Which function table shows values for the equation $y = x - 3$?

   A

y	x
5	2
7	4
9	6
11	8
13	10

   B

y	x
3	1
6	2
9	3
12	4
15	5

   C

y	x
2	5
4	7
5	8
8	11
10	13

   D

y	x
4	1
5	2
6	3
7	4
8	5

A Cello for Clare

Richmond, PA—Clare Bradford is only 10 years old, but she knows what she wants to be. "I want to be a cellist," she told the *Pittsburgh Post-Gazette*. Cellos come in different sizes. When Clare first learned to play, she played on a quarter-size cello.

About 2 years ago, her instructor knew she was ready for a half-size cello. He knew that to improve her playing, Clare needed a bigger cello. However, the cello he wanted for Clare cost $7,000—more than her family could afford. An anonymous donor heard of Clare. The donor decided that Clare had a lot of talent. The donor bought her the half-size cello so she could continue to play.

The Bradford house is filled with music. Her father is a musician, her older sister, Cecilia, plays the piano, and her younger sisters, Miriam and Emma, want to play the viola and violin.

Solve It

You can use equations to find the ages of Clare's sisters. Show your work on a separate sheet of paper. Remember, Clare is 10 years old.

1. Use the equation to find out how old Emma is.
   In the equation *e* stands for Emma's age and *a* stands for Clare's age.

   $e = a \div 2$ _____

2. Use the equation to find out how old Miriam is.
   In the equation *m* stands for Miriam's age and *a* stands for Clare's age.

   $m = a - 4$ _____

3. Use the equation to find out how old Cecilia is.
   In the equation *l* stands for Cecilia's age and *a* stands for Clare's age.

   $l = a + 3$ _____

Show What You Learned

Now that you have practiced working with functions and equations, take this quiz to show what you learned. Choose the letter of the correct answer for each problem.

1. Which number is missing from the function table?

Number of Cars	1	3	5	7	9
Number of Passengers	5	15	25	☐	45

A 26

B 30

C 35

D 55

2. Which equation represents the statement?

Gretchen is 5 inches taller than Marta (*m*). How tall is Gretchen (*t*)?

A $t = 5m$

B $t = m + 5$

C $t = m \div 5$

D $t = m - 5$

Use the function table for problems 3 and 4.

Number of Nests	Number of Chicks
3	6
6	☐
8	16
12	24
15	30

3. Which number is missing from the function table?

A 9

B 10

C 12

D 15

4. What is the rule for the table?

A The number of chicks is equal to the number of nests divided by 2.

B The number of chicks is equal to the number of nests plus 3.

C The number of chicks is equal to the number of nests minus 8.

D The number of chicks is equal to the number of nests times 2.

5. Which function table shows values for the equation $a = b \div 2$.

A

a	b
5	10
6	12
7	14
8	16
9	18

B

a	b
10	5
12	6
14	7
16	8
18	9

C

a	b
12	10
14	12
16	14
18	16
20	18

D

a	b
10	8
12	10
14	12
16	14
18	16

Use the situation below for problems 6 and 7.

A gardener plants 3 marigolds (*m*) for each snapdragon (*s*) she plants. How many marigolds does the gardener plant?

6. Which equation represents the situation?

 A $m = s \div 3$

 B $m = s + 3$

 C $m = s - 3$

 D $m = 3s$

7. If the gardener plants 9 snapdragons, how many marigolds does she plant?

 A 27 marigolds

 B 9 marigolds

 C 6 marigolds

 D 3 marigolds

Show your work on a separate sheet of paper.

8. Tickets for a movie cost $7 each. Write an equation you can use to find the cost for a group of people to go to the movies. Then, make a table of values for the equation for 1 to 6 people.

Show What You Know

Before you begin this lesson on mean, median, mode, and range, answer these questions. Choose the letter of the correct answer for each problem.

Use the line plot for problems 1 and 2.

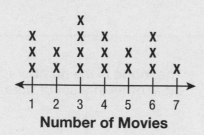

Number of Movies

1. What is the mode of the data?

   A 6

   B 4

   C 3

   D 2

2. What is the range of the data?

   A 6

   B 4

   C 3

   D 2

3. What is the median for the data set?

   18, 19, 20, 21, 21

   A 3

   B 19

   C 20

   D 21

Use the chart for problems 4–6.

Day	T-Shirts Sold
1	12
2	14
3	20
4	18
5	14
6	24

4. What is the range of the data?

   A 12

   B 14

   C 15

   D 16

5. What is the mode of the data?

   A 13

   B 14

   C 15

   D 16

6. What is the mean of the data?

   A 12

   B 14

   C 16

   D 17

You can describe data in different ways. You will learn to describe data using mean, median, mode, and range.

Here's How

What are the mode and range of the heights of fourth graders?

Think About It

You can use the data in the **line plot** to solve this problem.

The mode is the number found most often in a set of data.

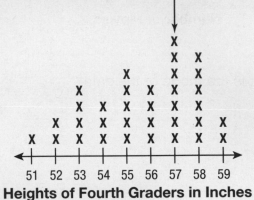

Heights of Fourth Graders in Inches

The **range** is the difference between the greatest number and least number in a data set.

greatest number − least number = range

$$59 \quad - \quad 51 \quad = \quad 8$$

So, the mode is 57 and the range is 8.

Try This Strategy

Find the Median
What is the median of the data set?
11, 13, 13, 14, 17, 19, 22

The **median** is the middle number in a group of numbers arranged in order.

11, 13, 13, **14**, 17, 19, 22

The median is 14.

Study the problem. Use the **Math Guide** for tips that can help you understand how to find the **mean** of a data set.

 Math Guide

The mean is sometimes called the average.

If you do not have connecting cubes, you can use counters or ones place-value models.

The stacks should all be the same height.

The soccer team played 4 games this week. They score 1, 4, 5, and 6 points during the games. What is the soccer team's mean score for the 4 games?

You can use connecting cubes to solve this problem.

Make stacks of cubes to model the number of points scored in each game.

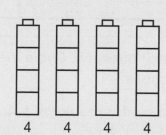

Rearrange the cubes so each stack has the same number of cubes.

Count the number of cubes in each stack. This is the mean. So, the mean score is 4 points.

Now, use what you already know and what you learned to find the **mean, median, mode, and range of data sets.**

Answer the questions on the next page.

Practice the Skill 1

Practice finding mean, median, mode, and range by solving the problems below.

EXAMPLE

What is the mean of the data set?

4, 5, 5, 6

A 2
B 4
C 5
D 6

What do you need to find?

Find the mean of the data set using connecting cubes.

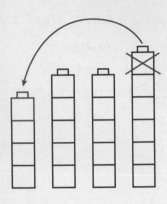

Now, read each question. Circle the letter of the correct answer. You may use connecting cubes.

Use this data set for problems 1–4.

3, 3, 4, 8, 12

1. What is the mode of the data set?

A 3
B 4
C 6
D 9

2. What is the range of the data set?

A 3
B 4
C 6
D 9

3. What is the median of the data set?

A 3
B 4
C 6
D 9

4. What is the mean of the data set?

A 3
B 4
C 6
D 9

GRIDIRON GIRL

Torrance, CA—The coach was happy with the football game. The quarterback completed four passes for three touchdowns. The team won the game! It was a normal high school football game—except that the quarterback was a girl.

Miranda McOsker is on her high school football team. During tryouts, she just wanted to make the team. But, when the coaches saw her throw, they asked her to try out for quarterback. Since then, Miranda has been playing quarterback.

Though it is unusual for a girl to play on a high school football team, Miranda's teammates think of her as just another player. Her parents also support her playing football. Miranda is glad to have a chance to enjoy her sport and play a game she loves with her friends.

Solve It

The data shows the number of touchdowns made by a high school football team during 5 games. Use the data to answer the questions. Show your work on a separate sheet of paper.

Touchdowns Scored
2, 2, 3, 4, 4

1. What is the median number of touchdowns scored? _____

2. What is the range of touchdowns scored? _____

3. What is the mean number of touchdowns scored? _____

Ladder to Success

Review

You have learned how to find mean, median, mode, and range.

Review the methods you can use to find mean, median, mode, and range.

- Order the data to help you find the median, the mode, and the range.
- Use connecting cubes to help you find the mean.

Practice 1

The list shows the number of minutes that the girls in Mr. Jenkins's class spent studying for the spelling test. What is the median number of minutes the girls spent studying?

15, 17, 17, 18, 19, 20, 21

Reread the problem to see what you need to do.
You need to find the median of the data set.

How can you find the median of a data set?
You need to find the middle number in a group of numbers arranged in order.

Circle the middle number.
15, 17, 17, 18, 19, 20, 21

The median number of minutes the girls spend studying is _____.

Use the data above for problems 1 and 2.

1. What is the mode of the data?

   A 15
   B 17
   C 18
   D 21

2. What is the range of the data?

   A 6
   B 7
   C 17
   D 18

Practice 2

The line plot shows the number of children in some families. What is the mode of the data?

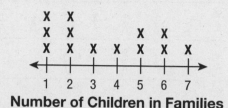

Number of Children in Families

Reread the problem to see what you need to do.
You need to find the mode of the data set.

How can you find the mode of a data set?
You need to find the number found most often in a data set. Sometimes, a data set has more than one mode. When this happens, you use both numbers as the modes.

On the line plot, look for the number of children with the greatest number of Xs.

The numbers that occur most often on the line plot

are _____ and _____.

The modes of the data set are _____ and _____.

Use the line plot above for problems 1 and 2.

1. What is the median of the data?

   A 2
   B 3
   C 6
   D 7

2. What is the range of the data?

   A 2
   B 4
   C 6
   D 7

Practice 3

The pictograph shows the number and type of pets owned by the students in Mrs. Rourke's fourth grade class. Find the mean, median, mode, and range for the data.

Student Pets

Dog	👤 👤 👤 👤 👤 👤 👤 👤 👤
Bird	👤 👤 👤 👤 👤 👤
Turtle	👤 👤
Cat	👤 👤 👤 👤
Fish	👤 👤 👤 👤

Key: Each 👤 is 1 vote.

Reread the problem to see what you need to do.

You need to find the mean, median, mode, and range for the data.

How can you use data from a pictograph?

First, find the number of votes for each pet from the pictograph.

Dog: 9   Bird: 6   Turtle: 2   Cat: 4   Fish: 4

Then, order the data from least to greatest.

2, 4, 4, 6, 9

You can now find the mean, median, mode, and range for the data.

The mode of the data is _____.

The median of the data is _____.

Find the range of the data.

_____ − _____ = _____

The range is _____.

Use connecting cubes to find the mean of the data.

The mean is _____.

Guided Instruction 2

You will build upon what you have learned in Part 1 by learning to solve more complex problems involving mean, median, mode, and range.

What are the mode and range of the temperatures?

Think About It

You can use what you know about mode and range to solve this problem.

Order the numbers from least to greatest. 65, 68, 71, 73, 73, 75

The mode is 73. It is the only temperature that occurs more than once.

Subtract to find the range.
75 − 65 = 10
The range is 10.

So, the mode is 73, and the range is 10.

City	Temperature (°F)
Glens Falls	73
Lake Meade	75
Greenmont	71
Hillsboro	68
Madison	65
Paulet	73

Try This Strategy

Find the Median

What is the median temperature? When a data set has an even number of numbers, find the 2 middle numbers, add them together, and divide by 2. The result is the median.

65, 68, **71**, **73**, 73, 75
71 + 73 = 144
144 ÷ 2 = 72

The median is 72.

Study the problem. Use the **Math Guide** for tips that can help you understand how to find the **mean** of a data set.

 Math Guide

Use the data from the chart to find the mean.

The chart shows the number of students who volunteered after school this week. What is the mean number of volunteers?

Day	Number of Volunteers
Monday	9
Tuesday	10
Wednesday	7
Thursday	11
Friday	8

You can check your work with connecting cubes.

Be sure to add all of the numbers together.

There are 5 addends. The number of addends depends on the data.

You could use connecting cubes to solve this problem, but you can also use paper and pencil to solve the problem.

First, add all of the numbers.
$9 + 10 + 7 + 11 + 8 = 45$

Then, divide the sum by the number of addends.
$45 \div 5 = 9$

So, the mean number of volunteers is 9.

Now, use what you already know and what you learned to find the **mean, median, mode, and range** of data sets.

Answer the questions on the next page.

Practice the Skill 2

Choose the correct answer.

Use the chart for problems 1–3.

Day	Hot Lunches Sold
1	11
2	12
3	16
4	11
5	15

Use the chart for problems 4–6.

Day	Tickets Sold
Monday	21
Tuesday	9
Wednesday	10
Thursday	8
Friday	14
Saturday	10

1. What is the range of the data?

   A 5
   B 11
   C 13
   D 16

2. What is the median of the data?

   A 5
   B 11
   C 12
   D 13

3. What is the mean of the data?

   A 10
   B 11
   C 12
   D 13

4. What is the mode of the data?

   A 8
   B 10
   C 12
   D 13

5. What is the range of the data?

   A 8
   B 10
   C 12
   D 13

6. What is the mean of the data?

   A 8
   B 10
   C 12
   D 13

LIFE AROUND AN UNDERSEA VOLCANO

La Jolla, CA—Scientists are studying a growing undersea volcano. The volcano is built by hot magma that erupts from the volcano. It cools when it reaches the water and builds up the volcano. Someday, the volcano may even reach above the ocean's surface.

Eels swim in the warm water around the edge of the volcano. The eels eat shrimp carried toward the volcano by the ocean current. However, the inside of the volcano is deadly for many sea creatures. The constant eruptions pollute the water. Some of the only living things found in the volcano are worms that can live in very polluted water.

Solve It

The data table shows the number of eels counted each hour near the underwater volcano. Use the data for the questions. Show your work on a separate sheet of paper.

Hour	1	2	3	4	5	6
Number of Eels	7	14	7	9	12	5

1. What is the mode of the data set? _____

2. What is the range of the data set? _____

3. What is the mean number of eels counted? _____

Show What You Learned

Now that you have practiced finding mean, median, mode, and range, take this quiz to show what you have learned. Choose the letter of the correct answer for each problem.

Use the line plot for problems 1 and 2.

Number of Books Read

1. What is the mode of the data?

   A 2

   B 3

   C 4

   D 6

2. What is the range of the data?

   A 2

   B 3

   C 4

   D 6

3. What is the median for the data set?

29, 14, 21, 15, 24

   A 14

   B 15

   C 16

   D 21

Use the pictograph for problems 4–6.

Favorite Color

Green	✏️ ✏️ ✏️
Blue	✏️ ✏️ ✏️ ✏️
Orange	✏️ ✏️ ✏️
Red	✏️ ✏️

Key: Each ✏️ stands for 1 vote.

4. What is the range of the data?

   A 2

   B 3

   C 4

   D 12

5. What is the median of the data?

   A 2

   B 3

   C 4

   D 12

6. What is the mean of the data?

   A 2

   B 3

   C 4

   D 12

Use the chart for problems 7–10.

Game	Points Scored
1	7
2	14
3	12
4	10
5	9
6	14

7. What is the range of the data?

   A 6
   B 7
   C 11
   D 14

8. What is the median of the data?

   A 6
   B 7
   C 11
   D 14

9. What is the mode of the data?

   A 6
   B 7
   C 11
   D 14

10. What is the mean of the data?

   A 6
   B 7
   C 11
   D 14

11. Sierra plays a game with her brother. In her last 4 turns, she has earned 6 points, 0 points, 4 points, and 2 points. What is the mean number of points she has earned?

   A 3 points
   B 4 points
   C 6 points
   D 12 points

Show your work on a separate sheet of paper.

12. Julie finds the mean, median, mode, and range of this data set: 10, 7, 5, 3, and 5. She then adds a 3 to the data set. Which measures will be changed by adding the 3 to the data set: the mean, median, mode, or range? Explain your reasoning.

Show What You Know

Before you begin this lesson on bar graphs, answer these questions. Choose the letter of the correct answer for each problem.

Use the graph below for problems 1 and 2.

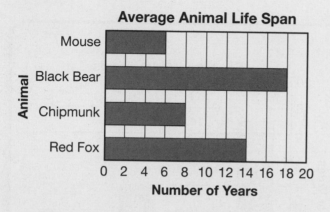

Average Animal Life Span

Use the graph below for problems 3 and 4.

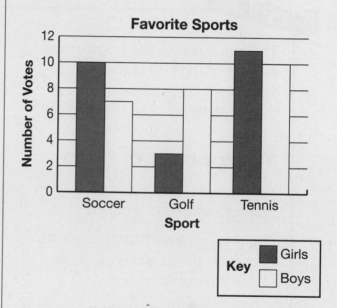

1. What is the average life span of a black bear?

   A 16 years
   B 17 years
   C 18 years
   D 19 years

2. How much longer is the average life span of a red fox than of a mouse?

   A 6 years
   B 8 years
   C 16 years
   D 20 years

3. How many boys and girls chose tennis as their favorite sport?

   A 1 student
   B 10 students
   C 19 students
   D 21 students

4. How many more boys than girls chose golf?

   A 8 more boys
   B 5 more boys
   C 4 more boys
   D 2 more boys

A **bar graph** shows data using bars of different lengths. In Part 1, you will study how to read, interpret, and make bar graphs.

Here's How

The graph shows the favorite wild animals of a group of students. How many more students chose the gorilla than chose the elephant?

Think About It

You can use data from the bar graph to solve this problem.

The graph shows that 12 students chose the gorilla and 8 students chose the elephant.

To find out how many more students chose the gorilla than chose the elephant, subtract.

$12 - 8 = 4$

So, 4 more students chose the gorilla than chose the elephant.

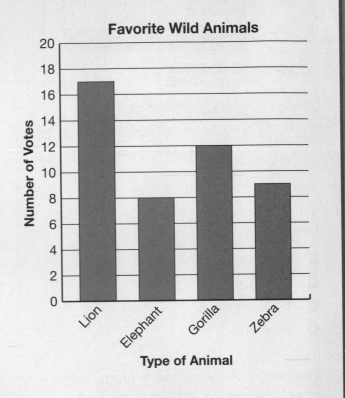

Favorite Wild Animals

Number of Votes (vertical axis, 0 to 20)

Type of Animal (horizontal axis: Lion, Elephant, Gorilla, Zebra)

Reading Data Between the Lines

On some bar graphs, bars may end halfway between 2 lines. When this occurs, the bar represents the number between the 2 lines.

How many students chose the lion?
The bar ends halfway between 16 and 18, which means that 17 students chose the lion.

Study the problem. Use the Math Guide for tips that can help you understand how to make a bar graph.

 **Math Guide**

Make a bar graph using the data in the table.

Favorite Fruits	
Type of Fruit	**Number of Votes**
Banana	14
Orange	7
Apple	19
Kiwi	2

Common **scales** to use include by 1s, 2s, 5s, and 10s.

Carefully label each side of the graph.

Make sure you are correctly plotting the data.

The title should clearly tell the topic of the graph.

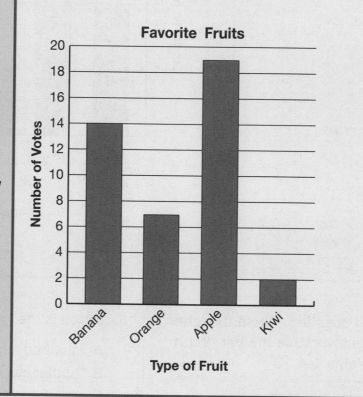

Now, use what you already know and what you learned to read and make bar graphs.

Answer the questions on the next page.

Practice the Skill 1

Practice reading and interpreting bar graphs by solving the problems below.

EXAMPLE

Which animal is 5 feet long?

A clouded leopard

B bottlenose dolphin

C horn shark

D puma

What do you need to find?

Find which animal is 5 feet long.

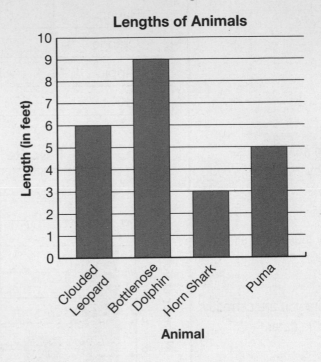

Lengths of Animals

The puma is 5 feet long.

Now, read each question. Circle the letter of the correct answer. Use the bar graph above for problems 1–4.

1. What is the length of a clouded leopard?

    A 5 feet   **C** 7 feet

    B 6 feet   **D** 8 feet

2. How many feet longer is a bottlenose dolphin than a horn shark?

    A 3 feet   **C** 6 feet

    B 5 feet   **D** 9 feet

3. Which is the longest animal?

    A clouded leopard

    B bottlenose dolphin

    C horn shark

    D puma

4. Which animal is 1 foot longer than the puma?

    A clouded leopard

    B bottlenose dolphin

    C horn shark

    D none of the above

NEWS FLASH!

Earth Is Warming

New York, NY—During the past 30 years, Earth has warmed more than 1 degree. This may seem like no big deal. But if it keeps getting warmer, it will affect all life on Earth.

As Earth gets warmer, the polar ice caps start to melt. This takes away places that plants and animals have to live. If they cannot find another place to live, they could die out.

Scientists hope to find more ways to keep Earth from warming. They study weather patterns. They also study how people change Earth. One way people can slow Earth's warming is to use fewer fossil fuels.

Solve It

Imagine you collect data about the average temperature in the Arctic. The table to the right shows the data collected. Make a bar graph to show the data. Show your work on a separate sheet of paper.

Average Arctic Temperature	
Day	Temperature (in °F)
Monday	5
Tuesday	7
Wednesday	4
Thursday	7

Answer the questions based on your graph.

1. Which 2 days had the same average temperature?

   _____

2. On what day was the temperature less than 5°F?

   _____

Review

You have learned how to read and make bar graphs.

Review the steps you can use to read and make bar graphs.

- Use the bar lengths to read and interpret bar graphs.
- Make bar graphs by choosing a scale and drawing bars.

Practice 1

How many students chose pizza for lunch?

School Lunch Sales

How can you find how many students chose pizza for lunch?

Read the data from the bar graph.

First, find pizza on the side of the graph.
Then, move across the graph until you find the end of the bar.
Then, move down to find the number of students.

Complete the statements below.

The bar ends halfway between _____ and _____.

The number halfway between _____ and _____ is _____.

How many students chose pizza for lunch? _____

Use the bar graph above for problems 1 and 2.

1. Which 2 lunch choices did the same number of students have?

   A salad and chicken   **C** salad and grilled cheese

   B pizza and salad   **D** pizza and grilled cheese

2. Which lunch choice did 45 students choose?

   A salad   **B** chicken   **C** pizza   **D** grilled cheese

Practice 2

The bar graph shows the number of books several students have checked out of the library. How many more books has LeAnn checked out than Harry?

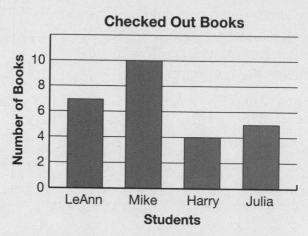

Checked Out Books

How can you find out how many more books LeAnn has checked out than Harry?

Read and interpret data from the bar graph.

How many books has LeAnn checked out? _____

How many books has Harry checked out? _____

Now, find the difference between the number of books.

LeAnn's books   −   Harry's books   =   difference

↓   ↓   ↓

☐   ☐   ☐

How many more books has LeAnn checked out than Harry? _____

Use the bar graph above for problems 1 and 2.

1. How many books have Mike and Julia checked out in all?

 A   5 books

 B   9 books

 C   14 books

 D   15 books

2. How many more books has LeAnn checked out than Julia?

 A   2 books

 B   4 books

 C   5 books

 D   7 books

Practice 3

Cody wrote down data from a survey in a table. He started to display the data in a bar graph but did not complete it. Complete the bar graph.

Favorite Colors	
Color	Number of Votes
Orange	25
Blue	30
Green	15
Red	45

How can you complete the bar graph?

First, draw and shade the rest of the bars. When you graph data that are between 2 numbers on the scale, end the bar halfway between the 2 numbers.

Then, give the graph a title.

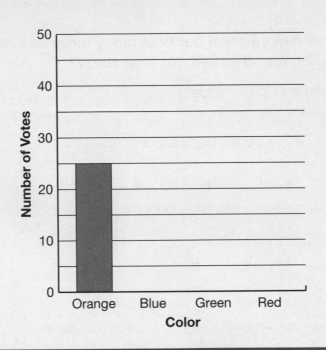

Use your completed bar graph to answer problems 1 and 2.

1. How can you tell which color most students chose by looking at your graph?

_____

_____

2. How many more students chose blue than chose green? _____

You will build upon what you learned in Part 1 as you learn to read and interpret **double-bar graphs** in Part 2.

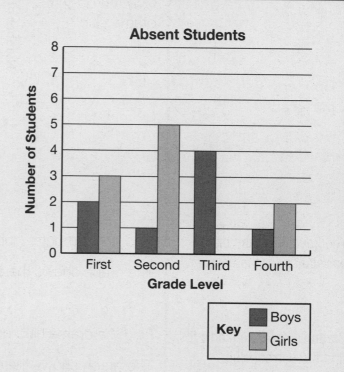

The graph shows the number of students absent at Greensboro School. How many girls were absent in fourth grade?

Think About It

You can use the double-bar graph to solve this problem.

Read the **key** at the bottom-right corner of the graph. The key shows the black bars stand for boys and the gray bars stand for girls. Since the question is about girls, you want to read the gray bars.

There were 2 girls absent in fourth grade.

Make Generalizations

When reading a double-bar graph, you can make generalizations about the data.

If you look at the double-bar graph above, you can make the generalization that more girls than boys were absent in first grade. You can make this generalization because you can quickly look at the graph and see the gray bar is taller than the black bar for first grade.

Study the problem. Use the **Math Guide** for tips that can help you understand how to read and interpret double-bar graphs to solve problems.

 Math Guide

You first read the data from the graph. Then, you will *interpret* it to answer the question.

How many more boys are in the computer club than in the drama club?

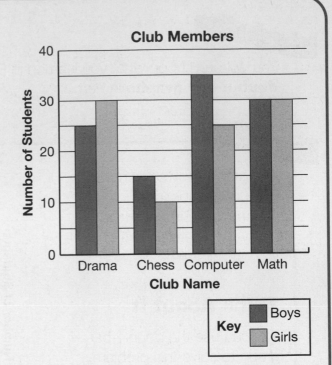

Club Members

Number of Students

Drama Chess Computer Math

Club Name

Key — Boys / Girls

The key shows the black bar stands for the boys.

Find the computer club on the bar graph.

The graph shows there are 35 boys in the computer club.

Carefully read the labels to find the correct club.

Find the drama club on the bar graph.

The graph shows there are 25 boys in the drama club.

Use the data. Read from the graph to solve the problem.

Find the difference between the number of boys in the computer club and the drama club.

35 boys − 25 boys = 10 boys

So, there are 10 more boys in the computer club than in the drama club.

Now, use what you already know and what you learned to **read and interpret double-bar graphs.**

Answer the questions on the next page.

Choose the correct answer. Use the bar graph below for problems 1–4.

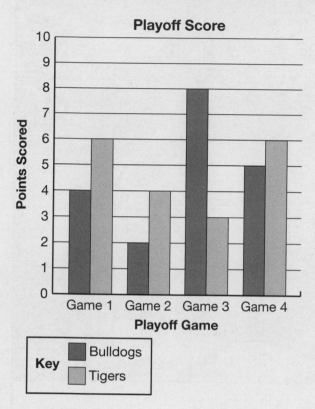

Playoff Score

Points Scored

Playoff Game

Key Bulldogs
     Tigers

1. How many points did the Tigers score in Game 2?

   A 6 points

   B 5 points

   C 4 points

   D 2 points

2. How many more points did the Tigers score than the Bulldogs in Game 1?

   A 5 points

   B 4 points

   C 3 points

   D 2 points

3. In which game did the Bulldogs score more points than the Tigers?

   A game 1

   B game 2

   C game 3

   D game 4

4. In which two games did the Tigers score 6 points?

   A game 1 and game 4

   B game 1 and game 2

   C game 2 and game 3

   D game 3 and game 4

NEED SNEAKERS?

Terschelling Island, The Netherlands—
Thousands of sneakers fell into the ocean and washed up on the shores of Terschelling Island. The sneakers fell into the ocean when nine containers fell off a cargo ship.

People were excited to scan the beach looking for a pair of sneakers. But they ran into a problem. The sneakers were not matched. So, a white size 10 sneaker could be next to a blue size 4 sneaker!

People were very happy to find a pair that matched in both size and color. Though some people also were happy with two sneakers that fit—even if they did not match.

Solve It

The double-bar graph shows some sneakers that washed up on the shore of Terschelling Island. Use the graph to answer the questions.

1. How many white size 7 sneakers washed onto the shore?

   _____

2. How many more black size 6 sneakers washed onto the shore than white size 6 sneakers?

   _____

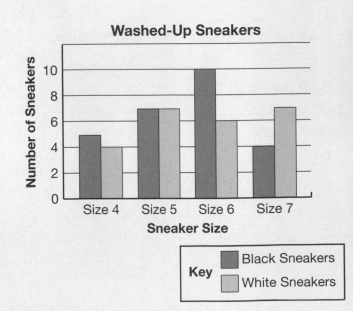

Washed-Up Sneakers

Number of Sneakers

Sneaker Size

Key — Black Sneakers / White Sneakers

Show What You Learned

Now that you have practiced reading and making bar graphs, take this quiz to show what you learned. Choose the letter of the correct answer for each problem.

Use the graph below for problems 1–4.

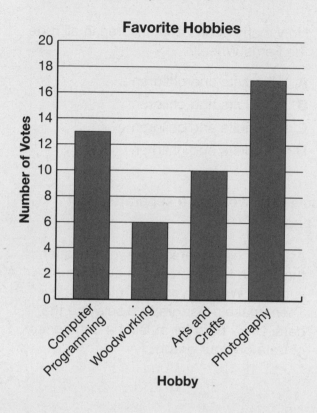

Favorite Hobbies

1. How many students chose photography as their favorite hobby?

   A 15 students

   B 16 students

   C 17 students

   D 18 students

2. How many more students chose computer programming than chose woodworking?

   A 13 students

   B 7 students

   C 6 students

   D 5 students

3. Which hobby did 4 fewer students choose than chose arts and crafts?

   A computer programming

   B woodworking

   C photography

   D none of the above

4. How many students chose either woodworking or computer programming as their favorite hobby?

   A 19 students

   B 18 students

   C 17 students

   D 16 students

Use the graph below for problems 5–7.

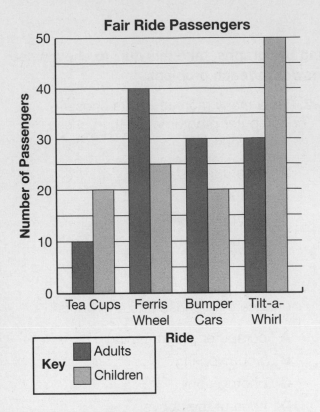

Fair Ride Passengers

Number of Passengers

Ride

Key — Adults / Children

5. How many more children than adults rode the Tilt-a-Whirl?

A 20 more children

B 30 more children

C 35 more children

D 40 more children

6. Which 2 rides did the same number of children ride?

A Tea Cups and Ferris Wheel

B Bumper Cars and Tilt-a-Whirl

C Tea Cups and Tilt-a-Whirl

D Tea Cups and Bumper Cars

7. How many adults and children in all rode the Ferris Wheel?

A 15 adults and children

B 60 adults and children

C 65 adults and children

D 70 adults and children

Show your work on a separate sheet of paper.

8. Ask your classmates a survey question that could be recorded on a bar graph, such as, What is your favorite color? Then, make a bar graph displaying the data. Draw bars for at least 4 categories of data on your graph.

Glossary

acute angle an angle that is less than a right angle (Lesson 7)

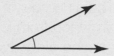

acute triangle a triangle with three acute angles (Lesson 7)

addition process used to combine or join groups (Lesson 3)

angle a figure formed by 2 rays that share an endpoint (Lesson 7)

area the measure, in square units, of the interior region of a two-dimensional figure (Lesson 6)

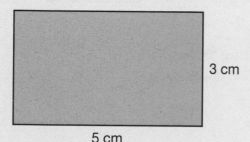

5 cm

3 cm

Area = 15 square centimeters (cm²)

bar graph a graph that shows data using bars of different heights (Lesson 10)

compatible numbers numbers that are close to the given numbers and easy to work with mentally (Lesson 2)

denominator the quantity below the bar in a fraction; it identifies the number of equal parts (Lesson 4 and Lesson 5)

difference the result of subtraction (Lesson 5)

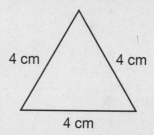

$$\frac{7}{8} - \frac{2}{8} = \frac{5}{8}$$

↑
difference

divide to separate into equal groups or to find how many in equal-sized groups (Lesson 2 and Lesson 3)

double-bar graph a graph that shows two sets of related data using bars of different heights (Lesson 10)

endpoint a point marking either end of a line segment or one end of a ray (Lesson 7)

equation a mathematical statement with an equal sign that shows two expressions are equal (Lesson 8)

equilateral triangle a triangle with three sides and angles that are equal (Lesson 7)

4 cm   4 cm

4 cm

equivalent fractions fractions that name the same number (Lesson 4 and Lesson 5)

Examples of equivalent fractions are $\frac{2}{3}$ and $\frac{4}{6}$.

expression a mathematical relationship that can be represented by variables, numbers, and symbols (Lesson 8)

factor a number that is multiplied to find a product (Lesson 1)

formula a mathematical statement or rule (Lesson 6)

fraction a quantity that names part of a whole or part of a group (Lesson 4)

$$\frac{1}{4}$$ ← numerator
← denominator

function a relation in which the value of 1 quantity depends on the value of another quantity (Lesson 8)

function table a table used to show the relationship between two quantities (Lesson 8)

greatest common factor (GCF) the greatest factor common to 2 or more numbers (Lesson 4)

inverse operations operations that undo one another; addition and subtraction are inverse operations; multiplication and division are inverse operations (Lesson 3)

isosceles triangle a triangle with two sides that are the same length (Lesson 7)

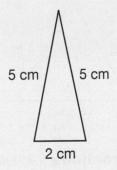

5 cm   5 cm

2 cm

key in double-bar graphs, a key tells what each type of bar stands for (Lesson 9 and Lesson 10)

least common denominator (LCD) the least whole number that is a multiple of the denominators of 2 or more fractions (Lesson 5)

length the distance along a line, figure, or object from one point to another (Lesson 6)

line plot a diagram that shows data using Xs above a number line (Lesson 9)

mean the sum of the numbers in a data set divided by the number of entries (Lesson 9)

median the middle number in a set when the values are arranged from least to greatest; or, the mean of the two middle values when the set has an even amount of numbers (Lesson 9)

mode the number that occurs most often in a set of data (Lesson 9)

multiple the product of a number and any whole number (Lesson 5)

multiply to find the total number of items made up of a given number of equal-sized groups (Lesson 1 and Lesson 3)

numerator the quantity above the bar in a fraction (Lesson 4 and Lesson 5)

obtuse angle an angle that is greater than a right angle (Lesson 7)

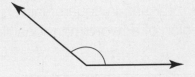

obtuse triangle a triangle with one obtuse angle (Lesson 7)

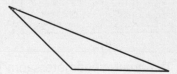

pattern a series of numbers or figures that follows a rule (Lesson 1, Lesson 2, Lesson 3, and Lesson 8)

perimeter the distance around a closed figure (Lesson 6)

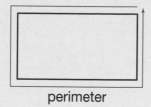

perimeter

product the result of multiplication (Lesson 1)

$$2 \times 5 = 10$$

product

quotient the result of division (Lesson 2)

$$15 \div 3 = 5$$

quotient

range the difference between the greatest value and the least value in a set of data (Lesson 9)

ray a line that has one endpoint and goes forever in 1 direction (Lesson 7)

rectangle a quadrilateral with both pairs of opposite sides parallel and equal and 4 right angles (Lesson 6)

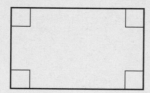

right angle an angle that measures exactly 90° (Lesson 7)

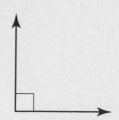

right triangle a triangle with exactly one right angle (Lesson 7)

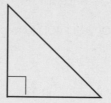

rule a statement describing a function (Lesson 8)

scale evenly spaced marks along the side of a graph (Lesson 10)

scalene triangle a triangle that has no sides or angles that are equal (Lesson 7)

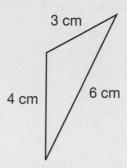

3 cm

4 cm   6 cm

side a line segment connected to other segments to form a polygon (Lesson 6 and Lesson 7)

simplest form a fraction whose numerator and denominator have no common factor greater than 1 (Lesson 4 and Lesson 5)

square a quadrilateral with 4 equal-length sides and 4 right angles (Lesson 6)

subtraction process used to find the difference between 2 numbers or to compare 2 numbers (Lesson 3)

sum the result of addition (Lesson 5)

$$\frac{1}{5} + \frac{2}{5} = \frac{3}{5}$$
$$\uparrow$$
$$\text{sum}$$

tree diagram a diagram showing the possible outcomes of an event (Lesson 3)

triangle a 3-sided polygon (Lesson 7)

variable a symbol used to represent a number or numbers; in 8x, the variable is x (Lesson 8)

width 1 dimension of a 2-dimensional figure (Lesson 6)

Math Tools

H	T	O

H	T	O

H	T	O

H	T	O

H	T	O

H	T	O

H	T	O

H	T	O

halves	$\frac{1}{2}$					$\frac{1}{2}$			

thirds	$\frac{1}{3}$		$\frac{1}{3}$			$\frac{1}{3}$			

fourths	$\frac{1}{4}$		$\frac{1}{4}$		$\frac{1}{4}$		$\frac{1}{4}$		

fifths	$\frac{1}{5}$		$\frac{1}{5}$		$\frac{1}{5}$		$\frac{1}{5}$		$\frac{1}{5}$

sixths	$\frac{1}{6}$	$\frac{1}{6}$	$\frac{1}{6}$	$\frac{1}{6}$	$\frac{1}{6}$	$\frac{1}{6}$			

eighths	$\frac{1}{8}$	$\frac{1}{8}$	$\frac{1}{8}$	$\frac{1}{8}$	$\frac{1}{8}$	$\frac{1}{8}$	$\frac{1}{8}$	$\frac{1}{8}$	

tenths	$\frac{1}{10}$	$\frac{1}{10}$	$\frac{1}{10}$	$\frac{1}{10}$	$\frac{1}{10}$	$\frac{1}{10}$	$\frac{1}{10}$	$\frac{1}{10}$	$\frac{1}{10}$	$\frac{1}{10}$

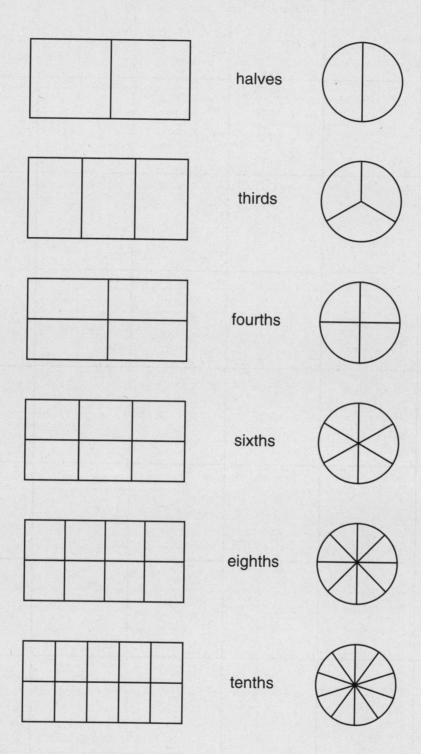

halves

thirds

fourths

sixths

eighths

tenths

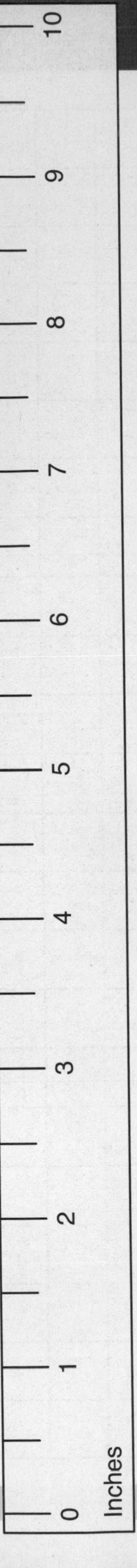

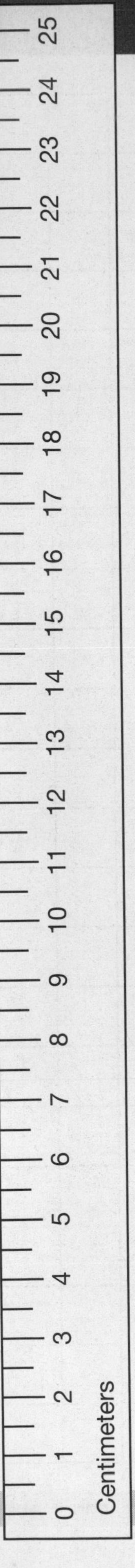

10
9
8
7
6
5
4
3
2
1
0

Inches

25
24
23
22
21
20
19
18
17
16
15
14
13
12
11
10
9
8
7
6
5
4
3
2
1
0

Centimeters

Remove Math Tools Here ◀

A **right angle** forms a square corner and measures exactly 90°.

An **acute angle** is less than a right angle.

An **obtuse angle** is greater than a right angle.

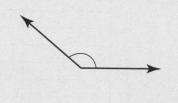

A **right triangle** has one right angle.

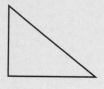

An **acute triangle** has three acute angles.

An **obtuse triangle** has one obtuse angle.

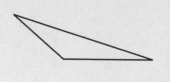

An **isosceles triangle** has at least two sides or angles that are equal.

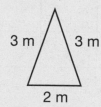

An **equilateral triangle** has three sides and angles that are equal.

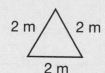

A **scalene triangle** has no sides or angles that are equal.

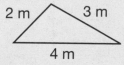

Vertical Bar Graph

Title:

(scale)

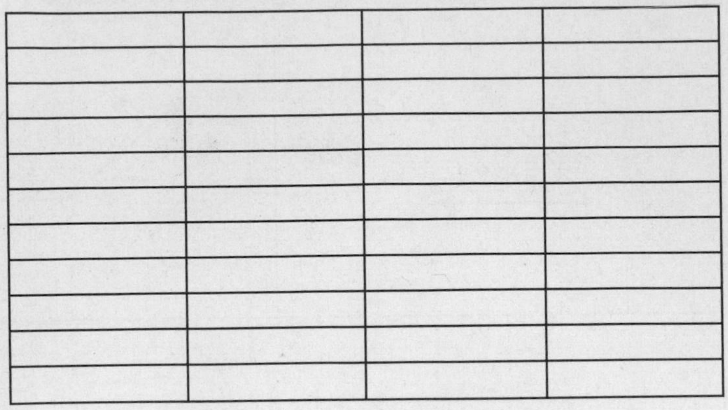

Horizontal Bar Graph

Title:

(scale)